Winelovers' handbook

Winelovers' handbook

by Pamela Vandyke Price
Editor of Wine & Food Magazine

SIMON AND SCHUSTER NEW YORK

Contents

Acknowledgments
Cover photograph by Barry Weller
Drawings by Roy Spencer, David Rushton,
Barney Wan, Barbara Firth
Maps by Edward Powers

Foreword

by H. W. Yoxall

In the course of a long life I have known few pleasures greater than the enjoyment of sound wine. Possibly I should have enjoyed most of it if I had known nothing about it; but the pleasure began to be greatly enhanced as I studied the subject and gradually got to know something about it.

The question is, Do you want to be a winelover, or merely a wine-drinker? If the former, love surely implies consideration of its object.

The things you really need to know are the various characteristics of the principal types of wine, which can be most readily memorized from the geography of the wine areas; and something about the care of wine, its service, and the appropriate matching of it to the accompanying food. But it will help to increase your appreciation if you can discriminate between the grapes that produce fine wine and those that produce *ordinaires*, and if you understand the general characteristics of the main methods of vinification.

All of the essentials for this fascinating and profitable study are set out, briefly and simply, in this *Winelovers' handbook*. Moreover, space is provided for recording impressions of the various bottles sampled – and it is most important to keep such records, for memories of taste are very evanescent. Intelligent comparisons of types of wine, vintages, optimum dates for consumption, and the styles of the different shippers, cannot be made by the average drinker without such written notes.

I have read many books on wine, but know none that will be more helpful than this to the aspirant winelover. It will also serve to remind the more experienced of much that he would otherwise have to search through numerous volumes to find. With its aid, and with that of the notes recorded in it – plus the advice of expert merchants, which is freely available to those who show interest – the reader will be equipped to receive the fullest gratification that the wonderful gift of wine affords.

H. W. Yoxall, OBE, MC, is a *Commandeur de la Confrérie des Chevaliers du Tastevin*, member of the Saintsbury Club, consultant to Wine & Food magazine, member of the management and executive committees of the International Wine and Food Society and author of *The Wines of Burgundy*, published by the Society.

About this book

This is a handbook for the winelover of today. There has never been one quite like it before.

In more spacious times, people ordered and laid down their wine in dozens at a time, recording their purchases and noting how the bottles tasted as they were drunk. A cellarbook of this sort is simple to keep – you merely need to rule off columns according to the name, vintage, source of supply and quantity of the wine, with any details of interest about its purchase and then enter your impressions of the wine's progress.

But this handbook has been planned for you, the contemporary wine drinker, who may have no more of a cellar than a rack holding a dozen bottles. You may wish to note impressions of wines tasted at tasting parties, as well as actually drunk at meals, or want to record details of wines sampled when you travel; you may need to annotate the wines on the lists of restaurants where you do more entertaining than at home, or want practical advice on buying, laying down, handling wines, and choosing the right ones to partner certain foods. Here is a conveniently-sized *aide mémoire* to the way in which the classic wines are made, a guide (with maps) to where they come from and the chief names to bear in mind. Of course, there are many excellent reference books on wine you can buy. But here is the essential information, both about wines and the way they should be used to get the most enjoyment from them, as well as the facilities for making your own notes side by side.

There is much that can be learned about wine. There is only one thing that need be – that its primary purpose is to be enjoyed. The wine drinker will find that a record of what, how, when he drinks can add enormously to his enjoyment in retrospect and encourage all kinds of experiments and adventures in wine for the future.

About wine

*Wine is a wonderful thing.
It is the subject for
much talk and
too much purple prose
but this is because
it is interesting
to those who love it,
not because it is
difficult to learn about.
The most important
thing to bear in mind
is that wine is meant
to be enjoyed.*

8

What is wine?

In 1936 the Wine and Spirit Association of Great Britain issued a definition which still applies throughout the United Kingdom: 'Wine is the alcoholic beverage obtained from the fermentation of the juice of freshly gathered grapes, the fermentation of which has been carried through in the district of origin and according to local tradition and practice.' The significance of this to the British wine drinker is that 'wine' as a term by itself is a beverage made from grapes, not other fruit or vegetables, and that it is made where those grapes have been grown. This is not a reflection on the quality of 'home made wines'; these can be very interesting and broaden the wine drinker's knowledge of the way the classic wines are produced.

Beverages which may have been made from 'musts' imported from other countries, or from dried grapes can also give pleasure to those who consume them. But it's wines in the definition's sense that all the nonsense is talked about – and it's these wines that can give many people the same kind of great pleasure as music, pictures, flowers, sport, and craftsmanship. Therefore it's worth knowing something about them.

Types of wine

The main types of wine are:
  table wines, red, white and rosé
  sparkling wines
  fortified wines
  vermouth and many apéritifs which are based on wine.
Although the processes by which the different types of wine are made vary considerably, the way in which grape juice becomes wine is in general the same. The juice of ripe grapes is extracted, either by crushing or pressing, and the yeasts on the bloom of the skin of the ripe fruit act on the unfermented grape juice (called 'must') so as to change it into alcohol and carbonic acid gas. The gas may be given off, during which time the wine bubbles and froths. Fermentation ceases either when the yeasts have used up all the sugar in the wine, or when the alcohol in the 'must' becomes sufficiently high in strength to check the process. Fermentation may also stop as the result of too high or too low a temperature, just as happens when one uses yeast for making bread. The majority of grapes, both white and black, yield pale yellow juice. In general, red wine is made from black grapes and white wine from white grapes, although some wines, notably Champagne, are made from a mixture of both.

The colour is usually given to red wines by allowing the skins of the black grapes to remain in contact with the 'must' for long enough to colour it. The time this takes varies according to the wine.

Vin rosé may be made either by leaving the skins of the black grapes in the 'must' for a short time, so as to tint it lightly, or by mixing red and white 'musts', or else by combining red and white wines.

White wine is usually made from white grapes, although it is perfectly possible to make a white wine from black grapes. As white wines get older, they have a tendency to deepen in colour.

Red wines also change colour with age, tending to lighten and become reddish brown, even tawny around the edge of the glass, as compared with the dark red, often purplish tone of a young wine.

Alcoholic strength

This cannot be judged by tasting – it is the concern of the wine chemist in the laboratory. The alcoholic strength of a wine influences the enjoyment of the wine as far as the drinker is concerned only in an indirect way, insofar as it is part of the constitution of the wine, rather as the skeleton of a beautiful person only concerns a doctor or a sculptor. The strength of different wines is controlled in the United Kingdom by the Customs and Excise, who levy duty according to a wine's alcoholic content, as to whether it is still or sparkling, and whether it is bottled in the country of its origin or in Britain.

Some wines seem to make more demands on the drinker than others, but this is not necessarily due to their alcoholic content. A wine may have a 'heady' fragrance, be very full-bodied and possess subtle qualities that take the attention. But it can be very light in alcohol as compared with, say, a carafe wine that has none of these characteristics, but which may be alcoholically stronger. The demands that a wine makes on the drinker are the result of its character, not its strength. It is more taxing to study a great work of art than a more trivial one. The strengths of different types of wines, as affecting Customs duties, fall onto the categories listed here, and are expressed in terms of percentage of alcohol by volume, a system known as Gay Lussac, after the man who evolved it.

Variations within the strength of still table wines may be considerable and it is worth reiterating that this cannot be detected by tasting. It should also be stressed that a wine that is a degree or so higher in alcohol is not necessarily a 'better' wine than one a few degrees lower. This depends on the type of wine. Some of the very finest Moselles, for example, tend to be low in alcoholic strength. The strength of a wine is very carefully watched by those who make it, in order to prepare it for its life (rather as doctors watch the bone structure develop in a human being), but this is something behind the wine, and not really the concern of the drinker who drinks for enjoyment.

Red, white and rosé table wines are between 7° to 14° (wine that is higher in alcoholic strength than 14° pays duty in Britain at the 'heavy' wine or fortified wine rate. Some wines from very sunny countries, where the climate results in the alcoholic content being high, often reach this point and present a problem to those who ship them).

Fortified wines are between 18° and 21°.

Vermouth and many apéritifs: between 16° and 20°.

Brandy of all kinds: between 45° and 55°. Occasionally brandies of comparatively low strength may be found, but these are exceptions.

Liqueurs and fruit cordials: 30° to 60°.

Still table wines

Wine making sounds a picturesque procedure, but it is as much a routine as potato lifting or hop picking. Most wines are made according to the procedure previously described.

When the 'must' has been changed into alcohol, the wines may be drawn off from the vat in which they were fermented, in which is left the residue of any bits of vegetation from the pressed grapes. The wine may then go either into vats or casks, depending both on the type it is, its quality and its individual life cycle. Sometimes a wine spends some time in a vat before going into cask, either for blending or for treatment; sometimes, as with many inexpensive wines, it may be bottled direct from the vat; sometimes it goes straight into cask.

Some of the greatest table wines spend an important part of their life (one to three years, but about two years as far as the majority are concerned) in wooden casks after they have been 'made' in the vat; during this time they mature until the moment arrives when they will benefit by going into bottle. The life of such wines continues in bottle, sometimes for as long or even longer than the life span of a human being. But for each wine there is, as in any life cycle, a period of youth and development, one of prime enjoyment, followed by a decline, which may be gradual or sudden.

An old wine is by no means invariably a better one than a young one. Many wines are at their best when young and fresh; only a few of the greatest contain within themselves the potentialities for long-term maturation in the right conditions.

Sparkling wines

There are several methods of making sparkling wine. The most famous is that by which Champagne is made and this, when applied to other wines, is usually indicated on the label. It is delicate, skilled and expensive, which is why wines made in this way cannot be cheap.

Each great Champagne house or other producer of wine subjected to the 'méthode Champenoise' will have certain characteristics produced by the variations in procedure peculiar to the establishment. But in general the wine is first made as a still wine is made, then bottled shortly after its vintage (often the following spring), when a type of secondary fermentation takes place. The carbon dioxide which would at that time be given off is held in the bottle, and it is this that gives the sparkle to the wine. The first cork in the bottle has to hold in the wine during its maturation and development. During this time the bottle is shaken from side to side and given a final slight turn while it is in an upside down position, throughout a period of months, so that any deposit that might form will slip down the bottle and come to rest on the cork. The first cork will then be taken out (a process known as 'dégorgement') when the wine is nearly ready to be offered for drinking. When the first cork and its deposit are removed, the wine may receive a sweetening (known as 'dosage') according to its style and the market for which it is destined. The bottle then receives its second cork and is 'dressed' (capsuled, labelled, etc.) ready to be sold.

A method which produces good sparkling wines on a large scale and at less cost than the Champagne process is known as 'cuve close' or the 'méthode Charmat'. In very general terms, the wine is put into a vat instead of into bottles and undergoes the process of secondary fermentation in this sealed vat. Afterwards, it is bottled in the ordinary way.

Certain types of wine – especially those that do not gain in quality by ageing – are just as suitable (in the opinion of some people even more so) to being subjected to the 'cuve close' process rather than the Champagne method. Wines produced by the 'cuve close' method are usually non-vintage and are most enjoyable drunk when young and fresh.

A recent development in the tradition of sparkling wines is a method by which, in very general terms, the first stage of the Champagne method is used, but, after the wine has been bottled, it is later disgorged into large tanks for treatment before being rebottled. This has certain advantages as regards the saving of cost and can also bestow the benefits of both methods on the wine. It is known in Germany as 'flaschengarerung' or, fermented in bottle.

Making sparkling wines by pumping carbon dioxide into them is a method never used for wines of any quality. It is unlikely that the British wine drinker will come across a wine made in this way – unless he wins a bottle of so-called 'Champagne' at a fairground on the Continent.

Fortified wines

The principal fortified wines are sherry, port and Madeira. All of these are higher in strength than table wines and each of them, as the name suggests, are 'made stronger' by the addition of brandy. In general terms, the brandy is added to the wine at different stages in its production. With sherry, the 'must' is allowed to complete its fermentation; with port, the fermentation process is arrested by the addition of the brandy. Brandy is added to Madeira when all the sugar that is not needed to give sweetness to the wine has been turned into alcohol, the amount varying according to the type of wine that is being made.

Cognac

Cognac is the world's supreme brandy. It can only be made within a specified area in the east of France, although brandy may be made from wine wherever wine is made.

The process of distillation can vary in detail but is basically the same; it is, however, these details and the base wine from which the distillation is made that determines the

ultimate product.

Cognac is distilled from the local wine of the region, which is very thin and harsh. It is made as wine in the ordinary way and then distilled twice, in a pot still, the beginnings and ends (known as 'heads and tails') of both distillations being put aside from the main distilled product. It is then put into wood – ideally into casks of Limousin oak – where it matures, and during which time a great deal of the brandy evaporates. As the Charente region, where Cognac is made, is fairly warm for most of the year, the evaporation is considerable (the producers say ruefully

'The sun is our best customer'), but the strength of the spirit in cask changes very little.

After a time the brandy is blended to make one of the great Cognacs according to the style of the house responsible. It is then bottled, after which time it ceases to improve, so that some of the vaunted 'old brandies' should be appraised solely with knowledge as to how long they have been kept in wood before being bottled. They will not improve indefinitely in cask, and after a while decline. The components of any great Cognac, however, may well be thirty to forty years old, or even possibly more. But dusty bottles mean nothing to anyone who really knows Cognac.

French law now prohibits the labelling of Cognac as the product of a single vintage but there is nothing to prevent the British wine merchant from buying an unblended Cognac of a particular vintage, shipping it to the United Kingdom and bottling it there when the time is ripe. There is a special style of Cognac known as 'old landed' not found anywhere else in the world; the Cognac so described will have been shipped in wood to a British bonded warehouse, where it will not have been 'refreshed' by being topped up (as inevitably happens in Cognac itself, when the brandy evaporates in the heat), and where the damp atmosphere of the cellars in the docks will slow down the evaporation and,

with the passage of time, the strength of the brandy may go down. Such Cognacs are not to everyone's taste, but those who like them, like them very much indeed.

Armagnac

The Armagnac region is in the south-east of France, near the Spanish frontier. Because Armagnac is distilled at a lower strength than Cognac, there is an erroneous idea that it is lower in alcoholic strength but of course the strength of a distillate of this kind can be made exactly to the requirements of the producer. In fact Armagnac and Cognac, in general, are of the same strength.

Serving wine

Attention to the details of serving wine can increase the enjoyment of drinking it, so care isn't mere chi-chi.

First and ideally, select wine for a meal twenty-four hours before it is required. If it is a red wine, stand it up where it is to be served, so that it may take on the temperature of the room, and so that any deposit may settle in the bottom of the bottle. An old white wine that may have thrown a deposit should also stand up to allow this to settle.

Opening bottles

A good corkscrew should be obtained, i.e. one with a spiral that does not end into a point going directly downwards – (this merely pierces the cork and may break it). Before opening any bottle, a cloth should be wrapped around the neck to guard against the possibility – slight but nevertheless existing – of the bottle breaking. Trim or remove the capsule so that the wine does not touch the metal when it is poured, wipe the top of the cork and the neck of the bottle with a clean cloth, then insert the corkscrew firmly through the length of the cork, which should be drawn gently, without jerking; any additional force required can be exerted by the hand holding the neck of the bottle pushing downwards, against the upward pull by the hand on the corkscrew.

When the cork is out, the neck of the bottle should again be wiped with a clean cloth before the wine is poured.
If the cork breaks off, gently reinsert the corkscrew to remove the rest. (A cork extractor with prongs is also helpful.) If it cannot be extracted, then push it down into the wine and any fragments of cork can be filtered off (see below).
If the bottle splits, the wine must of course be filtered. Do this either through a wine funnel fitted with a filter, a piece of filter paper, or completely clean linen – but nothing that has been washed in soapless detergent, or anything that may have been in contact with anything scented; this will inevitably affect the wine.

White and rosé wines (including the sparklers)

All of these should be served cold, but not so cold that the drinker is unable either to smell them or enjoy the flavour. Usually an hour in a refrigerator or about forty minutes in an ice bucket, filled with a mixture of ice and water, will chill the bottle for the wine inside to be refreshingly cool. Do not put wine into the deep freeze or keep bottles in the refrigerator; wines kept under refrigeration for more than a comparatively short space of time tend to go out of condition. If for some reason a bottle already in the refrigerator has not been used, put it in the least cold part and drink it as soon as possible. When using a bucket, make sure that the ice and water reaches up to the bottle neck. If, with tall bottles, this is impossible, put the bottle upside down in the bucket before drawing the cork. Thus the first glasses poured will be cool.

Sparkling wines
With one hand, hold a napkin around the bottle, remove the wire muzzle holding down the cork. From the moment the muzzle is removed, hold down the cork, then turn the bottle, *not* the cork, so that eventually the cork emerges from the bottle, making only a discreet noise. Throughout, keep the bottle at an angle, not upright or horizontal; this lessens the pressure behind the cork. A sparkling wine that has been subjected to shaking (if you have put it in the boot of a car for example) will have the pressure inside greatly increased and therefore the force with which the cork comes out will be very much greater. *Never* point a bottle of sparkling wine at anyone or at anything breakable.

If the cork is too tight to ease out, use Champagne pincers or lever the cork upwards with the thumbs. Should this still not work, hold the neck of the bottle for a few seconds under a stream of very hot water, holding the cork down all the while. The heat will cause a slight additional expansion in the wine inside the bottle, usually enough to force out the cork. Remember to hold on to it meanwhile.

If the top of the cork of a sparkling wine breaks off before it is drawn, pierce the cork with a skewer or thick needle so as to release some of the pressure inside the

bottle; then insert an ordinary corkscrew and draw the cork in the usual way.

Semi-sparkling wines
These should be opened like sparkling wines, although of course the pressure inside the bottle is not as great.

Fortified wines
Some of these may be fitted with crown corks (i.e. a metallic top to which a cork or plastic stopper is attached) or an entirely plastic stopper, thereby making the extraction and reinsertion of the stopper a simple matter. The neck of the bottles of the greatest fortified wines are slightly bulbous, and when these wines are old, as in the case of vintage port, the extraction of the cork can be a delicate matter. Ideally, the cork should be drawn exactly as for a table wine. But if with an aged wine there is the likelihood of the cork disintegrating, then either the wine must subsequently be poured through a filter, or else the neck of the bottle must be taken off. This is not really a difficult procedure, but it requires a certain knack. Ideally, one should see someone else do it first! (And practise with an empty bottle.)

There are two methods: one is to heat a special type of tongs until they are red hot. Then, wind a piece of wet cloth around the neck of the bottle and apply the tongs over this. After a few seconds the neck will crack and come off cleanly.

The other method is to insert a corkscrew gently but

firmly throughout the length of the cork. Then, with the back of a carving knife, chisel or similar narrow heavy instrument, and holding the corkscrew firmly with one hand, strike upward blows at the glass flange immediately below the top of the bottle, hitting all sides of it. Two smart blows should crack the neck of the bottle at this place, enabling the cork to be lifted off with the corkscrew. The crack should be clean and the wine can be decanted over the wiped cracked neck. All this is much easier to do once it has been demonstrated, and it is not as difficult as it probably sounds.

Pouring wine

Whether wine is poured from the bottle or decanted, it should never fill the glass by more than half or two-thirds. The space at the top of the glass enables the wine to be swirled round and for the drinker to enjoy the bouquet.

If, as the wine is poured, the bottle is turned slightly to one side and lifted when it is desired to stop pouring, the wine will not drip from the bottle. It is easiest to make this quarter turn clockwise if you are right handed.

Glasses and their care

There is a lot of affectation surrounding what salesmen often term 'suites' of glasses. Although many wine areas have glasses of a particular shape characteristic of the region, there is no need to use more than a single type of glass for any type of wine – still, sparkling or fortified. There are only a few essentials for a wine glass: it must be colourless, at least as far as the bowl is concerned, so that the colour of the wine is not hidden. It should be on a stem, so that, with white wines, the hand will not take the chill off the wine by grasping the bowl of the glass and, with all wines, so that the wine may be swirled around within the bowl of the glass and release its bouquet. The bowl of the glass should be either that of an elongated tulip, or like an onion with the top cut off – bulbous with the top of the bowl curving slightly inwards. This is the ideal shape for the presentation of the wine, its colour, its bouquet and its flavour.

A wine glass should be large enough to enable a reasonable portion of wine to be poured half or two-thirds up the bowl. In general, six to eight ounces is a reasonable size for all wines, although apéritif and fortified wines may be served in a four-ounce goblet. But a very small glass is only suitable for a digestive liqueur or a drink such as schnapps. Enormous glasses are mere gimmicks; the delicacy of a fine wine, especially one that is old, may receive too drastic aeration treatment by being swirled around in a goldfish bowl. The same applies to brandy balloons; they should not be of a larger size than can comfortably be cupped in one hand.

Although any sparkling wine may be served in goblets as described, the elongated flute shape, like an isosceles

1 *Glasses of a shape suitable for all red and white table wines, sparkling wines and fortified wines.* **2** *Traditional Champagne glass and glass ideal in shape for all sparkling wines.* **3** *Anjou wine glass and glass traditional on the Rhine, Moselle and in Alsace.* **4** *Glass for brandy and alcools blancs, small enough to be cupped in the hand, and copita or sherry glass.* **5** *Glass for digestive liqueurs and schnapps.*

triangle, is also suitable for sparkling wines, as it enables the bubbles to rise attractively and keeps the wine lively by providing maximum contact with the glass.

Deep Champagne saucers with hollow stems are attractive, though difficult to clean. Flat Champagne saucers encourage the wine to go flat, and are mean as regards helpings.

Glasses should always be spotlessly clean and it is usually necessary to polish them before using them, even if they have been put away after being polished. They should not be stored bowl down in a cupboard as they may then acquire a musty smell from having had the air shut up inside them. Store them upright. For wiping glasses never use a cloth that is going to be used for anything else – the glasses can take on the smell of anything that has even slightly tainted the cloth. If soap or detergent is used on wine glasses (very hot water alone is usually quite sufficient to clean them) then they must be thoroughly rinsed as this, too, can leave a smell behind it, and the presence of a detergent on a glass may not only affect the flavour of a wine, but can actually change its colour unattractively and take the sparkle out of sparkling wine. Glass cloths, when they are washed, should also be very thoroughly rinsed so that no trace of smell remains on them.

Decanting

This is not just an act to make you tip the wine waiter. There are several reasons why wines are decanted. The obvious one is to pour the wine – red *or* white – off any deposit that may have formed in it during its period of maturation. Then, the process of decanting brings the wine into the fresh air outside its bottle so that it can 'breathe' and get away from any staleness that is sometimes noticeable in the first glass of wine immediately after a bottle has been opened; this is the smell of the small quantity of air previously imprisoned in the bottle, which is known in wine talk as 'bottle stink'.

Contact with the air will often improve a red wine in many ways: a young, tough wine may have its roughness smoothed out by being exposed to the air. A very fine wine drunk (for some reason) before it has reached its prime, will be smoothed out by aeration and, if it is decanted some while ahead of when it is going to be drunk, it will give an impression of what it might be like when truly ready for drinking. If a wine seems dead and lifeless, the process of decanting very often revitalises it. And all red wines brought from a cold cellar will also be slightly warmed by being poured through the air into another container.

Some people do not like their wines decanted. The only way to decide is to take two bottles of the same wine, decant one an hour ahead of drinking time, and, later, merely draw the cork of the other; then see which is the most enjoyable. It is for you to make up your mind.

Decanting should be carried out with some source of light – candle, torch, bicycle lamp or unshielded electric bulb – in a position so that it illuminates the neck and shoulders of the bottle, either from underneath or transversely, so that any deposit may be seen the moment it moves up the bottle and the pouring can then be stopped.

Decanting is simple: whether a decanter, carafe, or another bottle is to be used to receive the wine, this should be sniffed to see that it is odourless before the pouring starts. (If a white wine is to be decanted, make sure that the decanter is chilled as well as the bottle of wine.) Wine should be poured slowly into the decanter, without the bottle being shaken or tilted up and down, and it should flow down the side of the decanter in a gradual stream, without splashing.

Decanters

These should always be clean and sweet and therefore it is advisable to wash them thoroughly immediately after they have been used, drain them and dry them off inside. Stale water inside a decanter can generate an unpleasant smell which has to be thoroughly rinsed away before the decanter can be used again. It is advisable to dry out the decanter with a cloth poked around inside, wrapped round a stick or skewer. If any wine stains adhere to the inside of the decanter, they can usually be lifted with a little ammonia, or tea leaves with vinegar, a little soda, or a few teaspoonfuls of Milton. When the stain has been removed, the decanter must be very thoroughly rinsed in clean water to remove any trace of the cleansing agent. A nuisance? Sometimes. But it is always less of a nuisance than a spoiled bottle.

Cradles

The use of the wine cradle, beloved of certain 'atmosphere' restaurants, should be restricted solely to carrying the bottle of wine from its recumbent position in the bin to where it is to be decanted. It remains lying down so that no deposit is disturbed, the cork can be drawn while it rests in the basket, and then, either the bottle is taken out and held, still at an angle, while the wine is decanted, or it may be poured from the basket. If a wine is suddenly required and has not been standing upright (so that any deposit has settled around the punt or base of the bottle), then the wine cradle or basket may be used to take the bottle from the bin, and any heavy deposit remains undisturbed. But as the slopping up and down of a bottle held and served in this way can stir up sediment far more than if the bottle is opened and poured with a steady hand from an upright and gradually inclined position, the use of the cradle should only be very occasional; with a really old bottle, in which the wine has thrown a heavy deposit, it is advisable to pour all the wine out at once, gradually inclining the bottle from glass to glass, not tipping the bottle up and down at all. This will do away with the risk of stirring up the deposit and, even if there are only two people drinking, it is better to have seven glasses of a star bright wine to drink from than only four or five, with the rest becoming muddy.

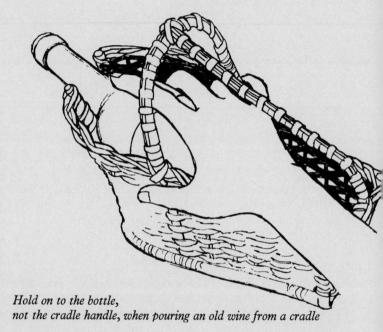

Hold on to the bottle,
not the cradle handle, when pouring an old wine from a cradle

Advice on the time at which wines should be decanted should be sought from a wine merchant, but in general most people consider that any young wine or a wine of medium quality will gain by being decanted an hour or more before the meal at which it is to be served, some great clarets benefiting by two or more hours airing. Wines more than fifteen to twenty years old may be a little more delicate and very old wines may have to be opened only immediately before the meal.

20

Choice of wine with food

There are few arbitrary rules about this, but until a little experience in wine drinking has been gained, there are certain combinations of food and drink that are generally the most enjoyable. Wines with a meal should be chosen either to complement or contrast with the food: this means that a very rich dish can be partnered by either a very full bodied and robust wine, or an extremely dry, crisp one. A superb but simple dish may be accompanied by a fairly light, delicate wine or else by a great wine. In general, the quality of the food and wine should usually be the same; consistency in this respect is important, because a very light delicate wine can be swamped if served with strongly seasoned regional food, and a tough everyday wine may spoil a very delicate dish.

Nothing particular is achieved by buying a wine of only everyday quality to accompany expensive food for a special occasion, but a single simple dish can be greatly enhanced by the choice of a good, even great bottle.

Order of serving: if more than one wine is served with a meal, serve a young wine before an older one, a dry wine before a sweet one, a delicate wine before one that is full or robust in character. Claret is usually served before Burgundy, unless a young Burgundy and an old claret are to be drunk, when a young wine will usually be more enjoyable first. White wines are usually more enjoyable before red wines, with the exception of the great white dessert wines, which usually come at the end of a meal. It should be borne in mind that the palate changes during the course of a meal, so that a series of wines should be considered in relation to the food served. For example, something very sweet will make anything even only medium dry, taken after it, taste almost unpleasantly dry, and even a medium dry wine taken after several rich dishes may give the impression of being thin and bitter. A very sweet wine, served early in the meal or before it, may cut the appetite instead of stimulating it, though there is no reason why sweet wines should not be served by way of apéritifs if the first course of the meal acts as a 'buffer state' between the sweet wine and anything dryer that is to follow.

With regional foods, it is ideal to serve the appropriate regional wine or the nearest equivalent.

One should remember that the palate will be changed by any drinks before the meal. If people are drinking several rounds of spirit-based cocktails, they will not be sensitive to the delicacies of a fine first-course wine. If the apéritifs are even slightly sweet, nothing too dry should come directly after them.

21

All purpose choice: if, as may happen in a restaurant, a variety of fish and meat dishes is ordered at once, a dry Champagne may accompany them throughout the meal, or any fairly full-bodied but dry white wine, such as a white Burgundy, or a wine similar in body and approximate dryness.

Salads: although a medium quality white, red or rosé wine *may* be served with any salad dish, the use of vinegar or lemon juice in the dressing can adversely affect the flavour of a fine wine. This is why a salad is usually served *after* a dish accompanied by wine in most wine-growing countries.

Chinese food: China tea ideally, or any all-purpose, medium-quality dry wine, still or pétillant.

Curry: Lager or, if wine is really required, anything inexpensive, either red or white.

Sauces: a rich or strongly-flavoured sauce can change the character of a dish, so that it requires a more robust wine to accompany it. It should be remembered that with a sauce including eggs, they can greatly and adversely affect the flavour of a delicate red wine.

Oysters: any dry white wine. Champagne for luxury occasions. Chablis, until it became very expensive, was the classic partner for oysters; now Muscadet is very popular, but any dry white wine, which is not too delicate in flavour, will do.

Caviare: dry Champagne or any good quality dry sparkling white wine, vodka or schnapps.

Hors d'oeuvre: there is no need to bother with a fine wine with a course like this, but you can serve a medium quality dry white wine, or a dry sherry if liked.

Smoked salmon and smoked fish in general: dry Champagne or a dry, but not too delicate white wine. There is much discussion as to whether there *is* a wine to partner smoked fish, but it is probably best to experiment and make up one's own mind. Many people like dry sherry, Madeira or white port, some might prefer no wine.

Foie gras and pâté: dry Champagne or a quality dry sparkling white wine, or a fairly full-bodied dry still wine. A coarse, highly-flavoured pâté needs a more robust wine, and a red wine might be acceptable with it. In the south-west of France the great sweet wines of Bordeaux are often served to partner foie gras but this is rather a specialized custom.

Melon: no wine necessary, but a glass of chilled tawny port, medium sherry or dry or medium Madeira if liked.

Soup: with clear soup serve the same sort of wine as for melon, but it is not necessary to serve anything with a cream soup.

Egg dishes: medium quality dry white, red or rosé wine. No fine wines with egg dishes but if either meat or fish is in the recipe, choose the wine to partner this.

Tasting wine

Although wine is a very wonderful thing to many people and an important article of commerce, it must never be forgotten that the only way in which to appraise it is according to the enjoyment it affords. Shippers and merchants have to anticipate the tastes of their customers when buying; the private individual need only consider his own taste and that of his friends. But it is essential never to confuse personal enthusiasm for a wine that one likes with an assessment of its quality; a wine may be first-rate in itself but less than pleasing in certain circumstances or to certain people. Usually, beginners find it easier to enjoy wines that have a little sweetness about them, but with experience the taste inevitably veers towards dryer wines. The preference for dry wines does not mean that they are 'better', only that in many circumstances they appear more immediately enjoyable.

It is essential to experiment with a wide range of wines, remembering, if possible, those liked and otherwise. If it helps the drinker to know something more about how the wine arrived in the bottle, this is fun, but it is not essential. It is always helpful to have the advice of any member of the wine trade in choosing wines, and this is a twofold traffic, for frankness as to how much may be spent and the occasion on which the wine is to be drunk will help the merchant in making the selection for his customers.

Wines that have won great reputations, and consequently command very high prices, are always worth studying. Indeed, the advice 'always drink something rather better than you can really afford' is sound, as it enables standards of quality to be established. But too much importance should never be attached to the label on the bottle or the price. Either by chance or carelessness, a wine that should be great may in fact sometimes be indifferent or even bad. Your own enjoyment is the prime standard – but it is always worth giving serious consideration to a wine that a large number of discriminating people sincerely enjoy.

It is not difficult to taste wine, but a different approach is used when tasting young wines in their country of origin before buying them, and tasting those that are ready to drink in the sort of tasting organized by a wine merchant or as a social function. But the basic procedure is the same: first, a small quantity of wine is poured into the glass and the colour is studied, ideally against a white background.

The wine should be clear and bright; as white wines get older they tend to darken in colour, and red wines become lighter and develop a curious tinge that, in extremes, is often described as 'brown'. In order to see the colour clearly, the glass may be tilted sideways.

The wine is then swirled around in the glass, so that the smell is released and may be sniffed. As the sense of taste is very largely a sense of smell, the 'nose' of a wine is an important indication as to what the wine is like.

A little wine is then taken into the mouth – for a critical

appraisal, far less than a mouthful that is to be drunk – and is allowed to run over the tongue and the sides of the mouth. It may then either be swallowed or spat out – there is usually some form of a spittoon at a serious tasting, or, for those tasting wines in cellars abroad, it is often permissible to spit on the floor. Spitting is essential when tasting young wines – they don't tempt you to drink them anyway – particularly if you have to go down a line of twenty or thirty and hope to arrive at the end still on your feet.

It is important to make any notes about the wines as soon as possible after tasting them, as first impressions remain vivid and enable the taster to recall the wine afterwards. It is not necessary to go into a lot of detail, but an immediate note is always helpful.

It is perfectly reasonable to expect to drink wines offered in a tasting given as a variation on a party, or by a wine merchant who is offering wines considered ready to drink.

If invited to taste in a wine trade tasting room, or on some occasion when someone is actually buying wine, it is obviously discourteous to distract the attention of the professional by smoking; women who are invited to taste in what may be described as a serious way should obviously not use scent immediately before tasting.

Tasting parties

These are easy to organize and a wine merchant will always help with advice as to the sort of wines to be shown and, if necessary, hire out glasses and offer other necessary equipment. For a party, it is advisable not to have too great a range of wines either in number or in scope; table wines are easier to taste in this way than fortified wines. Usually, some kind of unifying factor is advisable rather than just a range of different wines. For example, a selection of different wines of the same area or from the same vintage may be compared; wines of the same property of different vintages; wines of different regions within any of the classic areas, of the same vintage; wines of the same region and vintage shipped by different firms; wines made from the same grape but coming from different regions; fortified wines of the same type but from different houses; different sorts of vin rosé or sparkling wines, and so on. It is also best, in tasting of this kind, to keep to wines within approximately the same price range.

Points to bear in mind: space out the bottles so that people do not jostle each other at the tasting line and possibly cause spills. Ideally, have helpers to pour out a 'tasting portion' so that people do not waste wines (they can always come back for more). Have receptacles (empty bottles fitted with funnels) into which any unwanted wine may be poured away. If food other than chunks of cheese and biscuits is to be served, arrange this either in a separate room or at least away from the wines to be tasted. And, if the tasting is at all serious, put up at least one notice indicating 'No smoking'.

Storage of wine

Place

Ideally, wine should be stored – if for any length of time – in a place that is quiet, cool, dark and not anywhere very dry. Nor should the storage place also be used for anything with a strong smell; don't store your wines alongside fruit and vegetables, disinfectant and so on. Draughts – apart from adequate ventilation – are not ideal, nor is constant light, and if wine gets spilled or if open bottles are kept standing about, with the risk of their contents turning to vinegar, this can possibly contaminate even corked bottles.

If an actual cellar is not available, any quiet, darkish place, free from draughts, odours, and most important of all, sudden changes of temperature, will do. Part of a garage, empty coal or garden shed, a cupboard under the stairs (not in a centrally heated house), or loft (not directly under the roof or next to a heated tank), or a fitted cupboard, can all be adapted for storing wine. If there is really nowhere suitable, a wine merchant may be able to provide storage space, though the exigencies of our times usually require him to charge a small fee for this. Anyone with a real cellar can call on a merchant not merely to advise on the equipment of them, but to come and bin the wines for long-term storage.

Temperature

Direct heat and sudden changes of temperature are the enemies of wine. A temperature slightly above the ideal, but which remains constant, is preferable to one that may rise and fall throughout the year through more than a few degrees.

White wines should be kept cooler than red ones, if they are to be laid down for any length of time. In a small space they should be binned below the red wines, as heat rises. In very general terms, 45° – 48°F for white wines, 50° – 55°F for red wines is good, but slightly higher temperatures are unlikely to do serious harm, providing there is no substantial variation. Of course, wines can be kept perfectly well for three or four months even in a warmish place without deterioration, but they should not be changed about; once they have been brought from an ideal storage place, they should not be kept in a centrally heated building for several months and then returned to a cold cellar. The humidity of where they are kept also affects them; a damp cellar is in many ways better than a very dry one. But the main thing to bear in mind is that wines kept in a damp atmosphere (such as the great bonds at the docks) will mature more slowly than those kept anywhere at the same temperature, but dryer, and that, if they are labelled, their labels may be affected by the damp. Half bottles mature faster than bottles, and magnums more slowly.

1 *Square-shouldered Bordeaux bottle and half bottle, containing, like standard (75 cl.) wine bottles, about 8 and 4 glasses of wine.* 2 *Sloping-shouldered Burgundy bottle, a shape also used in the Rhône and for certain Loire wines.* 3 *Elongated bottle used for most German wines, usually brown in the Rhine and green in the Moselle.* 4 *Vintage port bottle.* 5 *Beaujolais 'pot' containing half a litre.* 6 *A clavelin used for many of the finer wines of the Jura region.* 7 *Champagne bottles: a half bottle; 3–4 glasses.* 8 *(a) Imperial pint; ¾ of a bottle. (b) A bottle; 6–7 glasses.* 9 *Magnum of Champagne or sparkling wine containing two bottles. A double magnum or Jeroboam of Champagne holds 4, but if it is of Bordeaux it holds 5. A Rehoboam holds 6, Methuselah 8, Salmanazar 12, Balthazar 16 and Nebuchadnezzar 20.* 10 *A Marie-Jeanne of the Loire, containing 1¾ bottles.* 11 *Chianti flask, holding 1 litre of wine.* 12 *Bocksbeutel, a flattish flagon-shaped bottle, used for steinwein from the region of Franconia in Germany.*

Laying down

Although a few of the finer great white wines are always worth laying down, it is the great red wines that are worth buying for consumption after a considerable period. This is due to several reasons: vintage port, claret and red Burgundy of certain years all have potentially very long lives and they can develop wonderfully if allowed the time to do so. The majority of white wines are most enjoyable when comparatively young and fresh, or at least within five to eight years, or not much more, of their vintages. There are exceptions, but these generally fall within the category of the top quality estate-bottled wines, about which the advice of an experienced merchant should be taken.

The life of the great red wines can, in exceptional years, be longer than that of humans. But as each year of the long-living vintages varies considerably, and as a wine that begins by being very hard and shows no apparent signs of softening and being ready for drinking for some time can very suddenly change and, after a short peak period, begin to decline, it is essential to have expert advice if one is to lay down wines of this sort for long-term drinking.

The following are rules of thumb, suppose one is presented with an unexpected chance of buying wine without having the chance to get a second and more informed opinion:

Vintage port: should not be touched for at least eight years after its vintage, ideally not for fifteen or twenty, and many vintages will only be beginning to show their quality at this stage. Certain 'off' vintages or light vintages may be enjoyable sooner. But if you are buying as an investment, vintage port is probably *the* blue chip, because the demand is great and, if the wine is properly kept, it will certainly appreciate in value even within ten years. When laying down vintage port, the important thing to remember is that the wine *must* have an initial period in which to form its crust – about five years. After this time, even if it has to be moved and even if it is actually shaken up, it can recover. If the crust is *not* formed in peace and quiet at the beginning, the wine is somehow never wholly satisfactory afterwards.

Red Burgundy: if buying for investment purposes, only domaine-bottlings will give a possibly good return in the event of a future re-sale. Certain very great years – and certain traditional producers – can achieve a wine that may live twenty to thirty years, but these are the exceptions nowadays. The greatest red Burgundies, of a very good or great year, will probably – if one can generalize at all about wine – be showing their quality at eight to ten years from their vintage, with a potential increase up to twelve, even fifteen years. The medium range will usually be at their best for up to eight or ten years. As the majority of red Burgundy is not domaine-bottled, the wines tend to mature more swiftly anyway. Small-scale Burgundies are intended for short-term drinking; ageing them will not make them better.

Red Bordeaux: known in Britain as claret, this is probably the longest-lived of all table wines. Even at a time when economic pressures make it necessary for many producers to adapt vinification methods so that wines are ready for drinking at a comparatively early stage in their lives, certain clarets of certain years (there may only be one vintage of this kind in a decade) will go on maturing and improving for twenty or thirty years. Estate-bottled wines tend to mature slightly more slowly than even the best of British bottlings and it is the former that should be bought if the wine is being purchased by way of investment and possible re-sale.

Certain of the greatest clarets, even in average years, should never be drunk before they are eight or ten years old; the 'light' years or 'off vintages' of the great properties are the wines that please at an early stage in their lives and are excellent for buying for short-term consumption.

In general, the first growths make wines that should never be drunk very young – they will seldom please; the classed growths of good – as differentiated from great – years tend to be at their best when they are more than ten, and possibly about fifteen or twenty years old; the bourgeois or lesser growths mature more quickly, but following the same lines, which makes them excellent 'controls' when laying down, if the buyer wants to keep an eye on the progress of a particular vintage.

Quantities: when laying down, it is advisable to buy sufficient bottles to ensure that a progressive experience of the wine can be enjoyed. Half bottles, maturing faster, enable sampling to be done before a whole bottle of a great wine is opened. Progress of wines should be watched and recorded by study of other people's drinking, by reference to one's wine merchant, and as a result of drawing from one's own cellar. For whereas a bottle that is opened too soon can, by judicious handling, be helped towards being better and indicating something of what it would have been if allowed to reach its prime (see page 19), a bottle that has gone 'over the top' can only be a source of regret and nothing can be done to improve it.

Some regulations affecting wine

With the growing interest in wine, many people nowadays concern themselves actively with procedures that they would otherwise have left entirely to their wine merchant.

Importing wine direct

There is nothing to prevent the holidaymaker buying a cask, or even less, of a wine still in wood and shipping it back to the U.K. to bottle himself. But the relevant permits have to be obtained and Customs procedure observed throughout, which may take a lot of time, especially for a small order. Similarly, it is possible to bottle one's own wine imported in this way, but, unless the correct equipment can be bought or borrowed and the wine handled with even a moderate amount of expertise, it may be spoiled. It is also worth noting that, on average, a cask of wine yields 282 bottles, which is a great deal of wine for a single small household to consume and therefore the procedure is seldom satisfactory long term, unless a number of people club together.

Wine may be imported in bottle, subject of course to the necessary regulations being observed. A wine merchant will often be able to arrange for the shipment of a small quantity of wine on behalf of a customer.

Resale

Wine is usually a good investment in the sense that fine wines, bought at the price at which they are first offered for sale, usually appreciate in value for some years. People who buy with the possible intention of selling at a profit later on, should bear the following in mind: without a licence, wine may not be offered for sale. It may be offered through the sale room (the auctioneer in this respect having the licence), or the wine merchant from whom it was purchased may take it back from the customer. But in neither case is the profit likely to be as high as will possibly have been expected. In the first instance, the salesman's commission has to be paid and, in sales anyway, prices may vary considerably according to the size of the lot offered; a wine merchant may not wish to handle a small quantity of wine, which is not worth putting on his list, and he will also probably have charged for it too. Wine may, of course, be sold privately between friends or to a restaurant where the customer is known, but strictly this is not in order. And, of course, if buying and selling of wine on a fairly large scale becomes a regular habit, the Inland Revenue authorities will also consider it as a source of income.

But in any event, the only sort of wines that are usually assured long-term investments – should someone be laying down a cellar for their heirs or with the view of putting aside small sums for the purchase of wines that could be sold again – are château-bottled clarets and vintage port.

With regard to any other wines, advice should be taken from a merchant experienced in these matters.

Bulk buying

People often join wine clubs because they are under the impression that they are buying advantageously. But it should be borne in mind that any wines bought in bulk (i.e. by the case) should usually gain a discount for the purchaser anyway; some clubs will not sell mixed case lots, and others require cash with the order to cut down book-keeping charges, so that these factors, plus possible delivery and/or storage charges, should all be taken into account. The question of the source of supply from which any club gets its wine is naturally of the highest importance, as the club has got to make its profits somewhere and may do this by offering spirits and certain branded lines at a negligible profit to itself, and cutting down on the quality of the table wines which may be less well known to the public.

Facilities that good clubs can offer, in addition to the actual wine they sell, often include news bulletins, tastings and special facilities for visiting abroad, though it is only fair to say that a good wine merchant can usually provide exactly the same services.

Anyone buying wines or spirits in quantities should get comparable quotations from several sources of supply.

Vintages in perspective

Age is not necessarily an advantage to a wine. Non-vintage wines are ready to be enjoyed immediately and won't benefit by keeping; wines such as Muscadet and the light, dry white wines of many countries whose charm is in their freshness, are most enjoyable drunk while young. White wines tend to age – and, consequently, decline – more quickly than red wines and they can darken in colour or 'maderise' as they do so; in outstanding years, certain great white wines may have long lives and the sweeter they are, the longer they can live,

but, generally, twenty years is a great age for a white wine – and it may be disappointing if kept.

Claret tends to have a longer life than red Burgundy, but much depends on the particular wine and its vintage; certain clarets can have a lifespan as long as that of a human being, but this is exceptional. 7–10 years is possibly a fair assessment of life for a fine claret in a lightish year, 12–15 for a good year, the 'little' clarets coming to maturity rather sooner than the classed growths.

Burgundies take less time and the wines of southern Burgundy will be ready earlier, usually, than the great wines of the Côte d'Or. Beaujolais is traditionally most enjoyable young and fresh.

Few vintage ports, even of light years, are drinkable before they are ten years old, most are best 15–20 years old or more.

Champagne is usually at its peak 7–15 years after its vintage, although some vintage Champagnes can live much longer. If the wine has been kept on its first cork – as can happen in the Champagne region – it can live a considerable time, but once it receives its second cork it begins to age and, eventually, to decline.

Half bottles mature more rapidly than bottles and magnums take longer to mature than bottles.

32

Wine regions of the world, details on page 49

Wines around the world

France

An enormous amount of wine is produced in France, both a variety of some of the finest table wines of the world and a great quantity of different wines of everyday quality. It should be borne in mind that to the Frenchman in general wine is a part of life and also possibly a matter of business, and that it is not often regarded with as much detailed appreciation or even knowledge as it may be accorded in other countries. Also, inhabitants of a region specializing in wine of a particular type will be inevitably partisan as regards this wine or group of wines; wines from other countries and even other regions will be of secondary interest.

The finest wines of France are produced and offered for sale according to the regulations of *appellation d'origine contrôlée*. These are determined by the local syndicates of wine growers and surveyed overall by a central authority, and in order to receive the A.O.C. the wine must comply with the local regulations as to:

the exact area where it is produced;

Vineyards around the world
The photographs on the previous pages show the variety of areas in which wine is grown and made. Page 33 California, page 34 Australia, page 35 South Africa, page 36 Switzerland, page 37 Austria, page 38 Cyprus, page 39 Spain, pages 40–42 Portugal, page 43 Italy, page 44 Germany, pages 45–48 France.

49

the type and density of grapes planted;

the minimum amount of sugar in the 'must' (the un-fermented grape juice);

the minimum degree of alcohol in the finished wine;

the maximum production of wine per hectare in hecto-litres (a hectolitre=22.4 gallons approximately);

the method of pruning and training of the vines.

An A.O.C. or A.C. is thus a type of pedigree for a wine, saying what it is and what it should be in relation to its ancestors, upbringing and capabilities. It is only by *implication* a certificate of quality, for it is perfectly possible to have a wine that is produced in strict conformity with the regulations from a vineyard or property enjoying a high reputation, that, for some perfectly good reason, is not particularly successful or may be lacking in quality. A.O.C. regulations only control the wines to the extent of where they come from and how they are made, the responsibility for their quality resting solely with the proprietors. At the same time, the granting of the appellation is very important and its possession highly prized.

In very general terms, the appellation referring to a vine-yard area or parish will be of higher standing than one merely referring to a more general area (e.g. a wine with the A.O.C. St. Julien will be higher than that with the A.O.C.

Médoc and this will be higher than the A.O.C. Bordeaux).

Beneath the A.C. wines come those marked V.D.Q.S. – *vins délimités de qualité supérieur* – each of which must have these letters on its label.

Below these come the *vins de consommation courante*, or the *ordinaires*. These may be branded wines, put out by many of the great wine houses for everyday drinking and these are known as *vins de marque*.

It should be stressed that although the majority of the regions of France produce wine, there are many of these which will not be found in wine lists outside that particular region. This may mean several things: the amount produced may be too small to warrant the cultivation of a market outside the area, or the type of wine may be such that so much care would be necessary to export it as to make the price uneconomic, or the character of the wine may be such that it is only suitable for consumption on its home ground. This is why holidaymakers who beg their wine merchants to import special wines they may have found while on their travels are often disappointed when it arrives. It should be stressed that, thanks to the shrewd buying and fair trading of the British wine trade, the United Kingdom enjoys a range of fine wines in all categories second to none in the world, and often at lower prices than the wines would cost in the country of their origin, especially France. This is why, unless you are actually staying in some great wine centre in France, it is always both more economic and more interesting to drink the local wines and not the great classics.

Alsace

The majority of Alsace wines are white and are named after the grape from which they are made: Riesling, Traminer, Gewürztraminer, Muscat, Pinot Blanc, Pinot Gris (also called Tokay d'Alsace) and Sylvaner.

If a wine is made from a blend of what are described as 'noble' grapes, it is called Edelzwicker. With other grape varieties involved, the blend can only be called Zwicker. There are several site names of which the best known are Kaefferkopf from Ammerschwihr, Sporen from Riquewihr and Brand from Turckheim.

Alsatian wines are usually at their best when drunk young and fresh. Occasionally a grower may make a wine from grapes gathered late, as in Germany, and this will be stated on the label. The different producers of wine put their names on their labels, and the difference between the style of, say, a Riesling from one firm and that of another, even from the same year, may be considerable and is always interesting.

Fruit brandies

Alsace is one of the great regions for fruit brandies, which are often served as digestives at the end of a rich meal. They are quite colourless, and not usually sweetened, so that the flavour of the fruit is strong. It is usual in Alsace to serve them in a glass previously filled with lumps of ice, swirled round to chill it, and then emptied before the brandy is poured in. This releases the bouquet. The main Alsatian fruit brandies are kirsch (cherry) and framboise (raspberry) which are possibly the two most famous of all, but others are made from fraise (strawberry), myrtille (billberry), sorbe alisier (a type of rowanberry), prunelle sauvage (sloe), mûre (blackberry), mirabelle (a type of small golden plum), and quetsch (another type of plum). A brandy called tutti-frutti is a mixture of fruits.

Beaujolais

The majority of Beaujolais is red, made from the Gamay grape. A little white Beaujolais is made nowadays. Beaujolais is usually drunk young and, when within a year of its vintage date, it is referred to as the 'vin de l'année'.

In addition to Beaujolais and Beaujolais Supérieur, there are Beaujolais Villages, the labels of which give the name of the village where the wine was made; there are also the main groups of Beaujolais, which are: Brouilly, Côtes de Brouilly, Chénas, Chiroubles, Fleurie, Juliénas, Morgon, Moulin-à-Vent, and Saint-Amour.

Occasionally a proprietor may add a site or property name to his Beaujolais.

Bordeaux

The Bordeaux region produces about one-third of all the quality wines of France. Both red and white wines are made in fairly equal quantities, there is some rosé and a little sparkling white wine. The principal grapes for red Bordeaux wines are Cabernet Franc, Cabernet Sauvignon, Merlot and Petit Verdot. For the white wines the grapes are Sauvignon, Sémillon and Muscadelle. The variety of the red wines, in all price ranges, is very great; the white wines include Sauternes, the greatest sweet wines of France, and many fine white wines both sweet and dry.

Properties

Although many Bordeaux wines are sold merely bearing the label of the parish or the general district in which they are made, the finer wines bear the name of the property producing them. The finest of all are referred to as 'classed growths' or *crus classés*, as each of the principal regions has classified or arranged its best wines in order of approximate merit. Of course, properties can change hands, methods of vinification alter and the general reputation of a wine may go up or down, so that the categorization of a wine in this way should not be accepted as absolute at any one time.

Médoc

The most famous classification of all was made of the red wine of the Médoc (together with one red Graves) in 1855, and although attempts have recently been made to change this, and some properties have virtually disappeared, the 1855 classification is still a fairly accurate assessment of the finest wines of the region. But one should never assume that, for example, a fifth classed growth is 'less good' than a third or even a second; all the classed growths are good and all are different. The first growths (with which Mouton-Rothschild is nowadays associated) do, however, achieve very high quality and their prices usually put them way ahead of the others.

The 1855 classification is as follows:

CHÂTEAUX	DISTRICT	CHÂTEAUX	DISTRICT
Premiers Crus		**Troisièmes Crus**	
Lafite	Pauillac	Kirwan	Cantenac
Margaux	Margaux	Issan	Cantenac
Latour	Pauillac	Lagrange	Saint Julien
Haut Brion	Pessac (Graves)	Langoa	Saint Julien
		Giscours	Labarde
Deuxièmes Crus		Malescot-Saint-Exupéry	Margaux
		Cantenac-Brown	Cantenac
Mouton-Rothschild	Pauillac	Palmer	Cantenac
Rausan-Ségla	Margaux	Grand la Lagune	Ludon
Rauzan-Gassies	Margaux	Desmirail	Margaux
Léoville-Lascases	Saint Julien	Calon-Ségur	Saint Estèphe
Léoville Poyferré	Saint Julien	Ferrière	Margaux
Léoville-Barton	Saint Julien	Marquis d'Alesme-Becker	Margaux
Durfort-Vivens	Margaux	Boyd-Cantenac	Margaux
Lascombes	Margaux		
Gruaud-Larose	Saint Julien	**Quatrièmes Crus**	
Brane-Cantenac	Cantenac		
Pichon-Longueville	Pauillac	Saint-Pierre-Sevaistre	Saint Julien
Pichon-Longueville-Lalande	Pauillac	Saint-Pierre-Bontemps	Saint Julien
Ducru-Beaucaillou	Saint Julien	Branaire-Ducru	Saint Julien
Cos d'Estournel	Saint Estèphe	Talbot	Saint Julien
Montrose	Saint Estèphe	Duhart-Milon	Pauillac

CHÂTEAUX	DISTRICT	CHÂTEAUX	DISTRICT
Poujet	Cantenac	Cos-Labory	Saint Estèphe
La Tour-Carnet	Saint Laurent	Clerc-Milon	Pauillac
Rochet	Saint Estèphe	Croizet-Bages	Pauillac
Beychevelle	Saint Julien	Cantemerle	Macau
Le Prieuré	Cantenac		
Marquis de Terme	Margaux		

The four first growths nowadays bottle all their wines at the château; other great properties sell some of their wine château bottled and some for merchants to bottle. Pontet Canet, the largest of all, never château bottles, and nor does Langoa-Barton (except of course, the wine for the personal cellars of the owners).

Cinquièmes Crus

CHÂTEAUX	DISTRICT
Pontet-Canet	Pauillac
Batailley	Pauillac
Haut-Batailley	Pauillac
Grand-Puy-Lacoste	Pauillac
Grand-Puy-Ducasse	Pauillac
Lynch-Bages	Pauillac
Lynch-Moussas	Pauillac
Dauzac	Labarde
Mouton-d'Armailhacq (now Mouton Baron Philippe)	Pauillac
La Tertre	Arsac
Haut-Bages-Libéral	Pauillac
Pédesclaux	Pauillac
Belgrave	Saint Laurent
Camensac	Saint Laurent

The other red wine producing districts,

apart from the Médoc, are:

Graves

The notable names here are:

Haut Brion

La Mission Haut Brion

Pape Clément

Domaine de Chevalier

Carbonnieux.

Several of these properties make fine white wines as well.

Saint-Émilion (and a range of sub-divisions)

(Ausone and Cheval Blanc are the two greatest wines)

Pomerol

(Pétrus)

Adjacent regions to Saint-Émilion are:

Néac; Lalande de Pomerol; Fronsac; Côtes de Canon Fronsac.

Good red wines also come from Bourg, Blaye and from the Premières Côtes de Bordeaux.

Below the hierarchy of the classed growths in the main areas come the bourgeois groups (many of which are nowadays of very high quality), then the artisan groups, and the wines bearing the names of small properties or just their district.

White Wines

The most famous area is that of Sauternes, which includes the district of Barsac, both of them producing the great sweet wines as the result of the action of what is called 'noble rot' on the skins of over-ripe grapes. The most famous Sauternes is Château Yquem, the two most famous Barsacs are Châteaux Coutet and Climens. The vineyards of Cérons, Loupiac and Sainte Croix du Mont also produce sweetish wines.

Graves, Entre-Deux-Mers, Premières Côtes de Bordeaux, Graves de Vayres and Blaye produce dryish wines.

Burgundy

Both dry white and red wines are made in Burgundy and, at their best, they rank among the finest of the world. Red Burgundies must be made from the Pinot grape; if the Pinot is mixed with the Gamay (the grape of the Beaujolais) the result is called 'Bourgogne Passe-Tout-Grains'. The finest white Burgundies are made from the Chardonnay and Pinot Blanc grapes; for the cheaper white wines, the Aligoté grape is used, and may be named on the wine's label.

Because the Burgundy vineyards are situated far enough north to be at the mercy of what can be severe climatic conditions, it is permitted to add a strictly controlled amount of sugar to the 'must' or unfermented grape juice when the wine is being made; otherwise the absence of sunshine and heat would greatly complicate the production of palatable wine in many years. This slight sweetening (known as 'chaptalization') is one of the reasons why Burgundy tends to be softer and slightly sweeter than claret. But fine Burgundy should never be 'heavy' or syrupy, either in bouquet or in taste and the finest wines have an elegance and velvety flavour that is beautiful. Although such wines can have long lives, even the finest Burgundies tend to reach their prime earlier than the great clarets and, as Burgundy is a smaller wine-producing region than Bordeaux, much less Burgundy is made. This means that, although there are plenty of good, and very many everyday

Burgundies, the greatest wines are always in short supply and tend to be costly. It is said that, whereas anyone who can afford the money can probably drink a fine claret several times a month, one's experience of the finest Burgundies may be limited to only a few in a lifetime.

With the exception of Chablis, somewhat removed from the main Burgundy region, and in the département of the Yonne, the finest red and white Burgundies come from the Côte d'Or, which stretches from just south of Beaune nearly to Dijon.

Chablis

Chablis, one of the most famous of white Burgundies, is the product of a small vineyard and the wines are never cheap. The main divisions of the Chablis wine are: Petit Chablis, Chablis (perhaps with the addition of 'premier cru' or the name of a vineyard), and Chablis Grand Cru. In the last category are certain of the great vineyards: Vaudésir, Preuses, Les Clos, Grenouilles, Bougros, Valmur, Blanchots.

Côte d'Or

The majority of the finest white wines, however, come from the Côte de Beaune within the region known as the Côte d'Or, and the majority of the finest reds from the Côte de Nuits, which stretches from north of Beaune nearly to Dijon. There are certain notable exceptions, and in a few vineyards both red and white wines are made, but in general the greatest whites (Montrachet and Meursault being the outstanding names) come from the region just south of Beaune, and the greatest reds (such as those from the tiny but world-renowned Romanée Conti vineyard, and those of Chambertin and Clos de Vougeot) from the Côte de Nuits. Immediately south of the Côte d'Or lie the Côtes Chalonnais and Mâconnais, both of them producing red and white wines; Mercurey, Givry, Rully, and Montagny are villages giving their names to wines in the former region, Pouilly Fuissé being perhaps the most famous wine name in the latter in addition to that of Mâcon itself.

The names of villages and towns important for their wines in the Côte de Beaune are: Aloxe-Corton, Savigny, Beaune, Volnay, Auxey-Duresses, Blagny, Puligny-Montrachet, Santenay, Pernand-Vergelesses, Chorey-les-Beaune, Pommard, Monthélie, Meursault, Saint-Aubin, Chassagne-Montrachet, Dezize-les-Maranges. Names of the Côte de Nuits villages are: Gevrey-Chambertin, Morey Saint Denis, Vougeot, Flagey-Echézeaux, Nuits Saint Georges, Fixin, Chambolle-Musigny, Vosne-Romanée. These regions give their names to the finest wines. In general, the use of a single name (such as Le Chambertin, Le Musigny, Le Corton, La Romanée) signifies a wine superior to the ordinary wine of the region. There are, as well, many vineyard names that are associated with the finest wines that do not always incorporate part of the village name with

theirs: Les Grèves, for example, is one of the fine vineyards of Beaune, Les Cailles of Nuits Saints Georges, Clos de Tart of Morey Saint Denis, La Tâche and Les Richebourg of Vosne-Romanée. But it should be remembered that the great vineyards of Burgundy are not – like those of Bordeaux – the property of a single owner or company; the Clos de Vougeot vineyard, for example, consists of plots split up between about sixty different owners. Each of the plot owners in a vineyard will make his wine in a slightly different way and each shipper will handle his wines in a slightly different way. Very little Burgundy is estate or domaine bottled, so that the wine of a single named vineyard, shipped by one firm, may differ considerably from a wine of exactly the same name and vintage, shipped by someone else. This is why it is important, when making notes of Burgundies tasted, to include the name of the proprietor of the particular portion of any named vineyard, and, always, the name of the firm who shipped the wine.

The Hospices de Beaune

The wines of the Hospices de Beaune are those belonging to the hospital and old people's home in Beaune, which has been supported since the 15th century by the products of the vineyards bequeathed to the Hospices. The sale of these wines in November attracts world-wide attention.

Throughout Burgundy some vin rosé is made and also sparkling wine, red, white and rosé.

Champagne

The Champagne region around Reims and Épernay is strictly delimited. Most of the wine is made from a mixture of black and white grapes, though some houses produce a 'Blanc de blancs', a wine made entirely from white grapes, which is very light and delicate. It is not necessarily 'better' Champagne, as the black grapes give body and fragrance to the wine.

For details as to how Champagne is made, see page 11.

The degree of sweetening varies from 'brut' or 'natur' (very little or no dosage of sweetening), 'extra dry', 'très sec', 'extra sec' (a little sweetening), 'dry' or 'sec' (slightly sweet), 'demi-sec' (sweet) and 'doux' (very sweet).

Vintage Champagne is made from a blend of the wines of a single vintage, to which may be added a little amount of vintage wine from another year if necessary. This is because the northern situation of the Champagne vineyards can make for extreme variations in the type and quality of wine produced. The bulk of Champagne is non-vintage, blended to ensure a continuity of quality from the enormous stocks of the Champagne houses.

Although there are many establishments producing Champagne, the leading houses are referred to as 'grandes marques'. The expression 'B.O.B.' means 'Buyer's own brand' and is the brand that a restaurant or a wine merchant may have made up specially to suit the demands of their own customers, with their own label. Pink Champagne is either Champagne in which the black grapes have been allowed to colour the 'must' at the time of the first fermentation, or else a careful blend of the red wine of the Champagne region with the white.

'Vin nature de la Champagne' is the still white wine of the region. It is seldom seen outside the Champagne district and at the present time its export is prohibited.

Loire

The Loire is a long river and a great variety of wines are produced along its banks and those of its tributaries. Farthest from the sea and almost in Burgundy are the vineyards of Pouilly and Sancerre. Wines entitled to the A.O.C. Pouilly-sur-Loire are made from the Chasselas grape. Those entitled to be called Pouilly Fumé or Blanc Fumé de Pouilly (the Blanc Fumé part refers to the grape, not the flavour of the wine), are made from a type of white Sauvignon. All these wines, together with those of Chavignol, Reuilly and Quincy, are white. There are various other pleasant local wines made throughout the château country. In Touraine, the red wines of Chinon, Bourgueil and Saint Nicolas de Bourgueil are notable, and vin rosé is made throughout most of this region and in Anjou. Any rosé described as 'Cabernet' will have been made from the Cabernet grape, one of the great claret grapes.

The château of Chenonceaux

Vouvray is both a still and a sparkling white wine; the white Saumur wines likewise. Some of them have site names as well as the regional name.

The Coteaux de l'Aubance wines are medium dry, those of the Coteaux du Layon rather sweet, Quart de Chaume being perhaps the best known. All are white wines. The Coteaux de la Loire white wines include the famous Coulée de Serrant, La Roche aux Moines and Savennières.

Near the sea, Muscadet is the most famous wine, made from a grape of the same name. There are three types entitled to an A.O.C. – Muscadet, Muscadet de Coteaux de la Loire, and Muscadet de Sèvre et Maine. Sometimes a bottle will be picked out as being 'sur lie'. This means that the wine will have been bottled just as it finishes its malo-lactic fermentation, while a high proportion of carbon dioxide remains in the wine, giving it a particular freshness.

In the Muscadet region also, there is a V.D.Q.S. wine, the Gros Plant, made from a grape of the same name.

Rhône

The Rhône vineyards fall into three main divisions: below Lyons, there is the Côte Rôtie which is divided into the Côte Brune and the Côte Blonde. The red wines are made from the Serine or Syrah grape and the white Viognier; this last is also used in the white wine of Condrieu. Most famous of the vineyards in this area is the tiny one of Château Gril-let, the only single property in France to have an A.O.C. to itself. Its wine is pinkish gold and of great individuality in flavour.

The second main division is comprised of the Côtes du Rhône vineyards which are situated on either side of the river around the towns of Tournon and Tain; both red and white wines are made, the Syrah being the grape of the former, the Marsanne and Roussanne for the latter. The vineyards of Crozes Hermitage and Hermitage are on the east bank; those of Saint Joseph, Cornas and Saint Péray (where a little sparkling wine is made) on the west bank, slightly farther to the south.

Châteauneuf du Pape

Châteauneuf du Pape, where great red wines and some fine white wines are made (the principal grapes being Grenache, Clairette, Syrah, Mourvèdre, Picpoul, Terret Noir, Picardin, Cinsault and Roussanne), is in the heart of a district which also produces other good wines, red, white and rosé, from districts such as Gigondas and Lirac which are now making names for themselves. Red and rosé wines are made on the mountain slopes of the Côtes de Ventoux.

In this region, too, is Tavel, possibly the most famous vin rosé of France, made chiefly from the Grenache grape, although several others are used.

Other wines of France

Wine is made in many other districts of France. Often, however, the local wines, though interesting and enjoyable to drink on their home ground, may not be suitable for exporting. Nowadays, with modern methods of vinification and preservation, this is not necessarily because they 'won't travel'; there may be only limited amounts made, so that it is not worth while developing markets outside the region, or the local demand may be sufficient to satisfy the producers.

It is always worth while drinking local wines, both because of their interest and because they will probably be less expensive where they are made than wines of other regions, even French ones. It should, however, be remembered that they are not usually meant to stand direct comparison with the great classic wines.

Germany

There are several main wine producing districts in Germany and within each an enormous variety of wines are made, so that any generalizations as to styles can only be approximate. Some of them command very high prices. The vineyards where the quality wines are made are seldom large and may be extremely difficult to cultivate, except by hand. The northern situation of the vineyards, too, presents them with the greatest hazards from adverse weather conditions.

The principal wine producing regions are: the **Rhine**, which is sub-divided into the vineyards of the Rheingau on the northern banks of the river and the Rheinhessen to the south and south-east of the river; the **Palatinate** or **Pfalz**, south of the Rheinhessen; the **Nahe** along the river of the same name to the south-west of the Rheingau. The wines of these districts are generally known as hock in the United Kingdom, but this is a purely English term. Nowadays, hocks are bottled in tall brown bottles. The **Mosel**, with its tributaries the Saar and Ruwer, is another of the main wine producing regions. Mosel wines are bottled in green bottles. **Franconia** is the region around Würzburg, the finest vineyards of which produce what is known as Steinwein, a term often used generally for all Franconian wines. They are bottled in a squat green flask known as a 'bocksbeutel'. Large quantities of wine, both red and white are made in the regions of Baden and Württemberg, much of it in the 'enjoyable everyday' quality rather than the very finest ranges.

The great quality grape of all the fine wines is the Riesling. Wines entitled to certain distinctive descriptions implying superior quality must be 100% Riesling. Other grape varieties in use are: Sylvaner, Traminer, Müller-Thurgau and Scheurebe. For the red wines, a variety of different grapes are used.

An enormous quantity of sparkling wine, generally referred to as 'Sekt', is made and consumed in Germany. These wines may bear the name of a region or even a property, or be blends, marketed under a brand name of the house producing them.

German wine names

People are sometimes intimidated by the long names they see on German wine labels, but in fact these are comparatively simple to understand. The inexpensive wines may merely be marketed under the name of the region producing them, with the suffix 'er', e.g. Niersteiner or Rüdesheimer, plus the vintage date and the name of the shipper. If the wine comes from a specific site, this will be mentioned after the general vineyard region, i.e. Bernkasteler Doktor,

Piesporter Goldtröpfchen. Following this, the grape may be mentioned (Riesling, Sylvaner, etc.) but this will usually only be done in the inexpensive ranges if it *is* the Riesling, the top quality grape, which is used.

Following the region, site and grape name, will be the indications of the particular quality of the wine, derived from the degree of ripeness and the way it was made.

The words 'naturrein', 'natur' or 'naturwein' imply that no additional sugar has been added to the 'must' when the wine has been made. This of course would not usually be done at all for the finer wines, so the term generally occurs only in the wines of medium quality.

The following terms occur frequently in the top quality ranges of German wines:

Spätlese: wine made from late-gathered grapes.

Auslese: wine made from specially selected bunches of grapes.

Beerenauslese: wine made from selected individual grapes which are over-ripe and on which the edelfaule, or noble rot, has produced the effect of seeming to wither the grape and concentrate the juice.

Trockenbeerenauslese: wine made from grapes which are affected by noble rot and dried so that they resemble raisins.

Eiswein: wine made from grapes actually frozen and pressed while the ice is still on them.

The above, going from spätlese to trockenbeerenauslese, indicate progressive degrees of sweetness and concentration in the wines. Eiswein may not be as sweet as a beerenauslese wine but will probably have some of the quality of the ripeness of an auslese.

The following words indicate estate bottling: Original-abfüllung, Wachstum, Kreszenz, Kellerabzug, Original-abzug, Kellerabfüllung. These will be followed by the name of the grower.

Cabinet or **Kabinett** implies 'special reserve'; the terms 'feine' and 'feinste' mean, respectively, fine and very fine, implying that, even for the fine wine ranges, this is a choice of what the grower considers to be a superior quality wine.

Sometimes the terms 'fass' and 'fuder' are included in the label, followed by a number. These refer to casks, as some of the finest wines are made and kept cask by cask, instead of being vatted together. Considerable difference is often perceptible between one cask and another.

Blends

In the inexpensive and medium ranges, shippers may make up blends of wines, either vintage or non-vintage, which they sell under brand names.

The most famous German wine is undoubtedly Liebfraumilch, which may be assumed to be a wine from the Rhine made in accordance with regulations to ensure a certain quality. Most shippers have their own Liebfraumilch and this may be vintage or non-vintage. It is essentially a wine blended to maintain the style and quality desired by the shipper, and varies very much, both as to type and price.

Italy

Italy produces an enormous number of wines of a varied nature in most parts of the country and also in Sardinia and Sicily. An important amount of wine production is concerned with vermouth, the centre of this industry being Turin. A variety of liqueurs and brandy are also made.

Italian wines sometimes take their name from the grapes from which they are made, although others are called after areas or towns. Production is becoming more controlled, but it is still generally true to say that a very large number of Italian wines are made for comparatively short-term maturation and for consumption on most everyday occasions. Certain wines do improve with keeping, but vintages are not often marked on labels, except for the very finest wines.

Very often the small-scale wine producer sells direct to his customers, so that the holiday-maker may encounter a huge variety of wines of different character, even when they all bear the same name and are on sale in cafés and restaurants within a comparatively small area.

Some of the best known table wines

Piedmont: Barolo; Barbaresco; Nebbiolo; Freisa; Barbera; Grignolino (all red). It is in Piedmont also that Asti Spumante is made from the Moscato grape. The process of making Asti usually combines part of the Champagne method and part of the 'cuve close' process. (Some spumante wines, made from the Pinot grape, are also produced entirely by the Champagne method.)

Liguria and Lombardy: white wines are produced at Cinque Terre, Vermentino, and on the shores of Lake Garda (Lugarno). Both red and white wines are made in the Valtellina valley.

The town of **Casteggio** is the centre of a district producing red, white and rosé wines called Frecciarossa.

Veneto: the region around Soave produces some of the best white wines of Italy bearing the same name. White wines are made in the Italian Tyrol under the name of Terlaner. Valpolicella from the Verona district and Bardolino from the east side of Lake Garda are the best known red wines.

Emilia: one of the best known wines is the red, slightly sparkling Lambrusco.

Tuscany: the most famous of all Italian wines comes from this district – Chianti. It is mostly red, though a white one is also made, strictly speaking not entitled to be described as 'Chianti'. Chianti Classico is the red wine from the defined area, but many good Chiantis are made outside of this. The very best quality Chiantis are not put up in the straw-covered flasks, but in bottles similar in shape to Bordeaux bottles in which they can be laid down to mature. The fermentation of Chianti involves the use of the 'governo', which roughly means that the wine has an additional fermentation induced by the addition of special 'must'. Wines made in this way have a very slight 'prickle', which should not be confused with any undesirable characteristics – it is something the Italians themselves like very much, though, out of consideration for the British taste, some of the Italian wines shipped to the U.K. are made without the use of the 'governo' because they are aimed, at least partly, at a non-Italian market.

Another red wine of Tuscany is Montepulciano. A sweet white wine called Vino Santo is also made.

Umbria: the most famous wine is the white Orvieto, in flasks which are not of litre size, but ordinary standard bottle capacity.

Lazio: the hills around Rome produce the wines of the Castelli Romani, some of them red, but most white, of

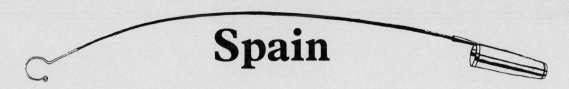

Spain

which the best-known is Frascati. Est, Est, Est is the name given to the white wines of Monte Fiascone.

Marche: this region produces some of the finest white Italian wines, including those of the Castelli di Jesi and Verdicchio.

Campania: around Naples, red and white Lacrima Christi is made, the best of which is white, and, rather unusually for a white wine, traditionally served at room temperature.

Ravello produces white and rosé wine: Gragnano a red wine and Falerno both red and white wine, of which the white is the better known.

The name 'Capri' is used for the white wines actually made from the Vesuvius district. Vesuvio is a red wine from the same district.

Marsala: this, Italy's most famous dessert wine, is made in Sicily. It is high strength and is made using processes similar to those involved in the production of sherry, port and Madeira. Marsala all' uovo is Marsala with which eggs have been incorporated.

The vast number of Italian wines makes it difficult to provide a basic directory, but in general it will be found that the best of the dry white wines come from the north or from mountainous districts.

The Italians do not usually observe any rigidity about red wine with meat or white wine with fish, and the majority of their wines combine pleasantly with all kinds of regional dishes.

Sherry

This fortified wine comes from a strictly delimited area around Jerez de la Frontera, Sanlucar de Barrameda and Puerto de Santa Maria. The principal grape is the Palomino; the Pedro Ximenez grape is also used for certain wines.

Sherry is a fully fermented wine, that is, the fermentation continues unchecked in any way until all the sugar in the 'must' has been converted into alcohol. Any sweetening is done by blending. All sherry is also produced in what is known as the 'solera' system, which, in very general terms, means that a number of wines of different ages, kept in cask in a bodega, are combined to produce the type of wine ultimately required. Although many of the wines in the solera may be of a great age, there is no vintage sherry made. Occasionally confusion occurs because of the belief of some that a particular sherry is not blended; there are some very fine sherries that come only from the wines of a single solera, without being blended with any others from outside at all. But all sherry is blended and all sherry is fortified with brandy, the amount of this varying very slightly because, in order to stand up to being transported, the shipping strength of a particularly fine sherry may be a degree or so higher than the strength at which the wine is offered for sale in Spain.

The bulk of sherry is imported in casks or containers, but a very little does get shipped in bottle.

The venencia, above, is used to draw sherry from the butt through the bung hole

Different styles of Sherry

There are two main types of sherry: fino and oloroso.

Finos develop a film of yeast cells on the surface of the wine in cask, and this is known as 'flor'. This is why the silver cup on a long handle, known as a 'venencia,' is used for taking sherry from the cask, because it enables the sampler to penetrate the surface covering of the 'flor' and draw up bright wine. Finos are the dryest of sherries and manzanilla, a type of fino, is very dry indeed; it is a fino from Sanlucar de Barrameda and is often supposed to have a slightly salty tang from the sea.

Amontillado sherry is a fino that has aged in wood and become softer and fuller in flavour, even slightly sweeter. Not all finos turn into amontillados with maturation, however. A true amontillado is not just a 'medium sherry' as is often assumed; it may be quite dry and often has a most beautiful nutty flavour.

Oloroso is a rather full-bodied and less delicate type of sherry, developed from what are called 'raya' wines while they are young. They do not grow 'flor' and would not ever have developed into finos or amontillados. Olorosos are often slightly soft in character and a darker gold than finos and amontillados, but they can be quite dry. A palo cortado is a special type of oloroso, although with their fresh bouquet these wines may seem to resemble amontillados.

The sweet sherries, usually marketed in the U.K. under such descriptive terms as 'milk' or 'cream', are made purely for the export market and are unknown in Spain. They can achieve great quality, especially if they are made up of old wines and allowed to mature for a considerable amount of time in bottle. They are frequently offered, like port and Madeira, as dessert wines, though of course they can be drunk at any time.

It must be appreciated that there is considerable difference, not merely between the basic types of sherries produced by the different sherry houses, but also between the range of wines within each separate category of each house. The date of a solera, sometimes put onto the label, indicates when the solera was founded and should not be confused with the age of the wine, which, as has been previously explained, is never the product of a single vintage.

Although in general there is no advantage in keeping a bottle of sherry once it has been bought, certain of the finest wines (a very small percentage indeed) are sometimes offered for sale as 'old bottled' and they will have changed their character slightly. A wine merchant will often put a date on such wines, indicating when they actually went into bottle. As far as other sherries are concerned, however, the sooner they are consumed after they have been bottled, the pleasanter they are. Sherry should *not* be left open indefinitely; after the bottle has been opened it is advisable to consume the delicate finos and manzanillas within a few days at least, although the fuller and sweeter wines will not suffer appreciably if the bottle or decanter is not finished

Stripping the bark from the cork trees

for a week or ten days.

Montilla: this district, north of the Jerez region, produces wines similar in style to sherry, although they cannot be sold as sherry. Although the wine is produced by the solera system, it is either only very slightly fortified or not at all. It was from the name 'montilla' that the word 'amontillado' evolved.

Table wines

Spain produces vast quantities of table wines, both red and white. The red wines in general probably achieve superior quality in the higher price ranges to the white wines, although in the medium and lower price ranges good wines in both categories are made.

Rioja is probably the best known Spanish red wine; the Priorato district in the province of Tarragona also produces quality red wines; in Valdepeñas, in New Castile, good red and white wines are made, notably around Don Quixote's home in the town of La Mancha. Much of the so-called Spanish Graves comes from the upper regions of the River Ebro, and the Spanish Sauternes type wines and Spanish Chablis type from Panades, also in the Province of Tarragona. Around Malaga are made rather sweet wines, once very popular in England, and in Tarragona, Valencia and Alicante sweetish red wines, sometimes slightly fortified, are also made. The famous sparkling white wine, Perelada, is made in Catalonia.

Portugal

Port

Port is considered by many to be the supreme dessert wine. It is made in a strictly defined area in the north of Portugal, around the upper reaches of the River Douro. A variety of grapes are used, both red and white. The vineyards are often very steeply terraced on the river banks, with a soil that resembles granite chips. The climate can be very extreme as regards both heat and cold.

The wine is made up country, the grapes being pressed either by the feet of workers in a rectangular stone trough called a lagar or, nowadays, by an electrically operated press. While the 'must' is fermenting, tests are continually made to ascertain the degree of sweetness and, when the required proportion has been reached, the process of fermentation is arrested by the addition of brandy. Later, the wine is taken down to the lodges of the port shippers in Vila Nova de Gaia, where the greater proportion will go into their blends. An ordinary port, matured in wood, will first be sold as ruby port; left to mature for a long time in wood, it will become paler in colour, change its flavour and be known as tawny port. The finest of the tawnies are exceptional wines, the product of long term maturing, but less expensive tawnies can be made by blending red and white port. White port is made from white grapes only; it is often drunk as an apéritif.

Vintage port is a very special wine, being blended from the wines of one outstanding year only, kept in wood for two or three years and then being bottled. It spends much of its life in bottle and will probably not be ready to drink before at least ten years after its vintage date and ideally not usually before fifteen years, though it should go on improving for much longer. It is up to the individual port house to decide whether or not to 'declare' a vintage and although in certain years all the shippers will declare, in others only a few may do so. The styles of the ports of the different houses are completely individual as far as all the wines are concerned.

Until recently, all vintage port was shipped in wood to the U.K. and bottled and matured there, but nowadays some vintage ports may be bottled in Portugal.

Because of its long life in bottle, vintage port requires an extra long cork of superior quality. It is also very important that, for the first five or six years of its life in bottle, it should not be moved, so that the wine may throw its 'crust', the heavy deposit that necessitates the port being decanted before it is to be served. Once this crust has formed, the wine can then be moved, if necessary, and even shaken up, providing of course that the crust is allowed to settle down once more over a period of weeks or months before the bottle is to be opened. One curious thing is that very often a year that may not be outstanding in any other of the classic wine regions of the northern hemisphere may be an outstanding one for vintage port.

Vintage character port is a blended wine of quality, that is ready for drinking once it is bottled.

Crusted port is a blend of quality wines that may have been kept for five or six years in cask before being bottled. If kept in bottle for some time, they will throw a crust and develop great quality.

Late bottled vintage is port of a single year, matured in wood for between three and six years and ready for drinking when bottled. It usually bears a vintage and a bottling date.

Table wines

Vinho verde: this 'green' wine comes from the Minho district in the north of Portugal, where the vines are trained very high. Both red and white are made, though it is the white wines that are probably best known. The production of all of them is subject to strict control. The character of the vinhos verdes is distinguished by the very slight sparkle

Oxen are still used to transport wine to the lodges

in them, produced by a form of fermentation known as malolactic, whereby a certain amount of carbon dioxide is retained in the wine. They are bottled in Portugal and, as they are meant to be drunk young and fresh, they do not bear vintage dates.

Other Portuguese table wines

There are a number of other good table wines made in Portugal: red and white Dão, red Colares, sweetish white Grandjo, and Setubal Muscadel; of these the two last are more in the style of dessert wines. A number of other wines

70

are also marketed under shippers' brand names or under the name of the property producing them.

Madeira

This wine is produced in the island of Madeira, from vines grown on trellises. There are four main types, called after the grapes from which they are made: Sercial, the dryest; Verdelho, which to some people has a slightly nutty flavour; Bual or Boal, golden brown and rather sweet; Malmsey or Malvasia, dark brown in colour and rich in flavour.

When the wine is made, the fermentation is either arrested (for the very sweet wines) or slowed down (for the drier wines) by the addition of brandy. Following this, the wine is subjected to being heated in rooms called 'estufas', over a period of time. The gradual raising and lowering of the temperature reproduces the effect of a sea voyage to the Far East, which in former times was found to improve the quality of Madeira enormously and for which purpose casks of the wine were used as ballast. Madeira then goes into a solera and is matured like sherry. Some of the Madeira houses make a special type of wine by blending and very occasionally vintage Madeiras are also made; the wine disputes with sherry the distinction of being the longest lived in the world and, although vintage Madeiras are not commercial propositions, it is by no means uncommon for wines of the 18th century to be drunk even at the present time.

Austria

A number of quality wines are made in Austria, the majority of them white. Grapes used include Riesling, Sauvignon, Traminer, Müller-Thurgau, Rotgipfler, Grüner Veltliner, and Muscat Ottonel. Some of the red wines are made from the St Laurent.

The main wine regions are: Lower Austria, where the majority of the wines are made, Burgenland, Styria and Vienna. There are some site names included among the wines exported to the U.K. and certain vintage descriptions, such as spätlese and auslese. There are also some 'perle' or very slightly sparkling wines made.

Switzerland

Although red and white wines are made in Switzerland, the majority of the wines of quality are white. The wine growing regions are: the Valais, Vaud, Neuchâtel, Geneva, the Ticino and Zurich.

The wines are made from a variety of grapes and the labels usually indicate the grape type. The white wines sometimes have a slight sparkle, the 'Star of Neuchâtel' being the most famous of these. The best-known red wine is called Dôle.

Yugoslavia

Some of the Yugoslav wines come from what are claimed to be the oldest wine producing areas in Europe. The main regions are: Slovenia (in which the famous districts of Lutomer, Maribor and Brda are situated), the River Sava, the shores of the Gulf of Trieste, where are found some of the red wines; Bosnia and Herzogovina, Serbia, Macedonia Dalmatia, Vojvodina.

Grape varieties include Riesling, Sylvaner, Pinot, Ruländer, Muscat, Zilavka and Furmint. Among the red wine grapes are: Prokupac, Cabernet, Brda, Merlot and Pinot Noir.

Rosé is also made.

Liqueurs and fruit brandies (of which the most famous is Slivowitz, made from blue plums) are also made.

Hungary

A variety of table wines are made in Hungary, the majority of the quality wines being white, although the famous Bull's Blood of Eger is red.

The principal region for quality wines is around Lake Balaton; Mor, near Budapest, Eger, Tokay and Somlo are other important wine regions.

The grape varieties include Riesling, Furmint, Traminer, Sylvaner, Muscadine, Veltellini, Szurkebarat, Kadarka, Harslevelü and the native grapes, the Kövidinka, Szlanka-mentha, and Sarfeher.

Tokay is the most famous Hungarian wine of dessert character. There is a dry type, but the most famous is a sweet dessert wine, bottled in half-litre bottles. The quality of the wine is characterized by the number of 'puttony', the name for the measure of the juice of over-ripe grapes. The number of puttonyos indicates the sugar content. In exceptional years Tokay essence, made from over-ripe specially selected grapes, may be made.

Other Balkan wines

Table wines of fair quality are made in Czechoslovakia, Rumania and Bulgaria. Most of them are white, but some are red and the Bulgarian red wines can achieve definite distinction.

Vintage dates are seldom given on Balkan wines, the majority of which are ready for drinking when, or soon after, they are bottled. In the United Kingdom they are usually sold under the brand names of those who ship them.

Luxembourg

In proportion to its size, Luxembourg produces a large quantity of white wines, made from the Riesling, Traminer, Ruländer and Auxerrois grapes; most of them are at their best when drunk comparatively young.

Cyprus

The island produces an enormous variety of wines, one-fifth of the population being engaged in the wine business.

A great deal of brandy is produced and a variety of fortified wines as well as table wines. Those in the former category coming to the United Kingdom are mostly Cyprus sherries, some of them being made with 'flor'. Other wines in the same style are produced by blending, some of them medium dry but a large quantity sweet.

Table wines

Red, white and rosé table wines are produced in Cyprus, the height of the mountain vineyards enabling dry white wines to be made. The chief grape for the white wines is the Xynisteri; for the red wines the black Mavron. There is also some vin rosé made. The wines usually bear Cypriot names.

Commandaria: this, the wine drunk by the Crusaders, is dark brown, very sweet, made from a blend of red and white grapes dried in the sun, and which reaches about 27° in strength. It is matured in earthenware jars and is capable of a very long life, like others of the great dessert wines.

North Africa

Most of the North African countries produce a variety of wines and also brandy. Those from Algeria have long been known in the United Kingdom and others from Morocco and Tunis are gaining in popularity. They are usually sold under the brand name of the shipper although visitors to North Africa may find certain estate wines.

In general, it is the red wines that are most successful in the United Kingdom markets, as their low price, soft, full-bodied character and easy appeal gain them a large following. The white wines usually come into the category of pleasant holiday drinks. Sparkling wines are also made.

South Africa

South Africa produces fortified wines, every kind of table wine and brandy. It is the South African sherries that have won particular reputation in the U.K., although the white table wines are increasing enormously in popularity.

Some South African wines are named after the European wines they are thought to resemble in character, especially when they are imported in bulk by large concerns marketing them under their own labels, but there are also a number of estate wines available in the U.K. which are sold under the names of their estates, sometimes with the grape variety added.

The regions of the Cape, where the wines are produced, are the coastal district and the Little Karoo.

Grape varieties include many of those used in the European classic vineyards, and there is also an indigenous variety called 'Steen' or 'Stein' from which quality table wines are made.

The South African wine farmers formed a Co-Operative Growers' Association in 1918. This, the Ko-Operative Wijnbouwers Vereniging, usually shortened to its initials, K.W.V., is the controlling body of the South African wine business and is responsible for the maintenance of quality in all ranges of the wines.

British drinkers of fortified wines from South Africa (or Australia) should be reminded that, due to a preferential system of duty, fortified wines from the Commonwealth countries only pay light wine duty on being imported into the U.K. Their local price on the British market is therefore advantageous to the drinker and not an exact indication of where they stand as regards quality in relation to fortified wines from other sources.

Australia

*Wineries in
the Barossa Valley*

A wide range of wines is made in Australia; fortified, table wines, still, sparkling and semi-sparkling wines and brandy.

Many of the great wine-growing estates produce a complete range of all wines, made from a wide variety of the grapes used in the European vineyards. Although vast quantities of Australian wines and spirits are exported, some of the very finest will only be found in Australia, as demand for them on the spot does not permit a surplus for export.

The majority of Australian wines still tend to be named according to the type of European wine that they are thought to resemble, however slightly, i.e. hock, Burgundy, claret and so on. Recently, however, the use by certain of the great Australian wine houses of their own brand and estate names, is beginning to establish greater individuality for the wines in the minds of the general public. The names of the shippers are consequently of great importance, as the type of wine made by one house will vary considerably from that of another.

The main Australian wine-producing regions are in the states of South Australia, New South Wales, Victoria, Western Australia and Queensland.

British drinkers of fortified wines from Australia should be reminded that the same preferential system of duty as that for South Africa is applicable.

USA

California

The most important and prolific wine-producing region of the United States is California. Vines have been cultivated there since about the 16th century and nowadays every kind of wine – table wines, fortified wines, sparkling wines, apéritifs and spirits – are made. Although few of these wines find their way to Europe, they are very well worth while sampling by anyone visiting the U.S.A., the medium range wines being good everyday drinking by any standards and the best wines being very good indeed. Many of the long-established properties' owners are descended from European wine-growing families and traditional practices, as well as the most up-to-date methods, are employed in wine production.

The grapes used in wine making are either the same strains as those of the classic vineyards elsewhere, or varieties of these, although one, the Zinfandel, used for red wine, will probably be unfamiliar to Europeans; it is difficult to trace as regards origin and, by now anyway, is virtually an 'American' grape. The wines are often marketed under the names of the grapes from which they are made, these being described as 'varietals'. All the vines are grafted, as elsewhere.

The principal Californian wine regions are: North Coast, Sacramento, the Central region, the San Joaquin Valley, and the South Coast. Each one uses a great variety of grapes and produces a wide variety of wines, some wineries producing a complete range of red, white, rosé, sparkling and apéritif wines.

The North Coast districts are Sonoma-Mendicino, Napa Solano, Livermore-Contra Costa, and Santa Clara-San Benito-Santa Cruz. Some of the finest table wines come from these areas, and many of the estates are famous, including the Buena Vista vineyards in the Sonoma Valley, Korbel in the Russian River Valley, the vineyards of Charles Krug, Beaulieu, the Christian Brothers, Louis Martini, Inglenook and Beringer in the Napa Valley, Wente and Colcannon in the Livermore Valley, Hallcrest in Santa Cruz, Almadén, San Martin, Hallcrest and Martin Rey in Santa Clara.

The Sacramento Valley produces a great deal of dessert and apéritif wine.

The Central region produces enormous quantities of table wines, the majority of these being of everyday quality.

The San Joaquin Valley wines include both table wines and dessert wines, the latter often being very good.

The South Coast wines tend to be light in character, and include a wide range of still and sparkling table wines.

A tremendous amount of sparkling wines, red, white and rosé, are made in California and, if they are produced according to the Champagne method, they can, according to law, be described on their labels as 'Champagne', although this would not be permitted in France or the U.K. They must, however, bear in addition the name of the place where they are made. The 'cuve close' method is also used and good sparkling wines are made by this process and, according to certain variations on the basic method, some outstanding technological advances have been achieved. Cheap sparkling wines are made by pumping carbon dioxide into the wine, and these must be sold under the description 'carbonated'.

The enormous variety of Californian wines make it difficult for the visitor to distinguish more than a few of them during the course of only a short stay, or in a few tastings, although visits to vineyards and wineries are encouraged and routes in the wine-growing regions are planned so that tours are easy. What is of great importance, for the wine lover accustomed to certain classic European wines, is to approach these and other American wines with an open mind and not be disconcerted by the use of grape names or styles of wines that are already familiar; in many instances, the blend of grapes used will be quite different from that used in a European vineyard, or a single grape only may be employed, when elsewhere several would be required. And, of course, differences in climate, soil and methods of vinification contribute to a great many differences in the final wine, with the additional factor that even the oldest of these vineyards tend to be young in comparison with many of the European 'classics'. All this adds to the interest they provide.

The European visitor, too, should bear in mind that it is not usual to find stocks of very old wines offered for sale in the U.S.A. Wineries tend to sell their wines when they are bottled, and stores, which may have few facilities for keeping stocks to mature, then offer them to the public. This means that, unless one is fortunate enough to be the guest of a wine estate, to discover a stock of old wines in some hotel or restaurant, or visit a private house that has a real 'cellar', it is difficult to appraise many of the best red wines, which may be still far from their prime. But of course they can provide much enjoyment, and the dry white and many of the quality sparkling white wines, of the type that is most pleasant when drunk young and fresh, are delightful. It is significant that, per head of the population, America drinks more wine annually than Britain.

New York State

New York State is second to California as the country's largest wine producer. Although California provides 85% of all American wines, New York makes more than half the sparkling wines, and the total output of wine – sparkling, table and dessert – from the 400 square mile wine-growing area is about 12½ million gallons a year.

In 1829 the Reverend William Bostwick planted American vines, brought from his previous parish in the Hudson River Valley, in the rectory garden of Hammondsport's Episcopal Church. The townspeople followed his example, planting vineyards on the shores of Lake Keuka, where the geography and climate proved to be ideal. As a result, two of the great American wineries were started here in the 1860s, and the other two major New York companies were set up about thirty years later.

European wine grapes do not thrive in the eastern United States, because of the very cold winters and problems of disease. The numerous different species of wild native grapes which flourish there are the basis of the wine industry. By cross-breeding these varieties, a new generation of hybrids, stronger and more prolific than their wild parents, has been evolved, although these wild grapes give a distinct taste to the wine, referred to as 'foxy' or 'goût sauvage'. A way of eliminating this has only recently been perfected however, mainly due to the efforts of Doctor Konstantin Frank, who has succeeded in grafting the buds of European wine grapes onto American roots.

The wineries concentrate mainly on the culture of grapes that are little known outside America, such as Concord, Catawba, Delaware, Dutchess, Elvira and Niagara, although some of the more important vineyards also grow Johannis-

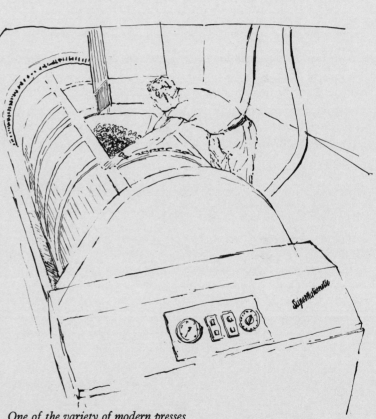

One of the variety of modern presses

berger Riesling, Chardonnay, Pinot noir quite successfully.

The Taylor wineries are the largest 'champagne' producers in the United States and also, like the Pleasant Valley wineries, produce a full range of wines. The premium 'champagne' of the Urbana estates is Charles Fournier Brut, and their Gold Seal Pinot Chardonnay and Gold Seal Johannisberg Riesling Spätlese are very good wines. The Widmer estate is smaller than these three wineries, but it produces 100% varietals and a unique 'sherry' that is left in its barrels on the roof for a minimum of four years before bottling.

Besides the Finger Lakes district, there are wineries at Batavia, Lewiston, in and around New York City, and at scattered points throughout the State.

Other American wine areas of importance are situated in Ohio, Maryland, Michigan, New Jersey and Washington. The wines are often labelled according to the grape variety used (the term employed is varietal), plus the name of the shipper. Many of the classic European wine grapes are employed, plus some hybrids.

Comparatively few American wines are available in the U.K. at the present time, as the inevitable high price in this market makes them a source of interest rather than a commercial proposition. Those that are imported include all types of still and sparkling table wines.

80

For further reading

There are many excellent books for the wine lover and space only permits the naming of a few, but several of the following contain bibliographies to encourage additional research. We have included only books covering the subject of wine in general:

A Wine Primer (Michael Joseph) and the **Concise Encyclopaedia of Gastronomy** (Wine & Food Society) – André L. Simon

A Guide to Good Wine – various authors, all members of the wine trade (Chambers)

The Penguin Book of Wines – Allan Sichel (Penguin)

An Alphabet of Choosing and Serving Wines and **The Home Wine Cellar** – Raymond Postgate (Herbert Jenkins)

Encyclopaedia of Wine – Frank Schoonmaker (Nelson, U.K.; Hastings House, U.S.A.)

Wines and Spirits of the World – edited by Alec Gold (Virtue)

Alexis Lichine's Encyclopaedia of Wines & Spirits (Cassell, U.K.; Alfred A. Knopf, U.S.A.)

Red, White and Rosé – Edmund Penning-Rowsell (Pan)

Wine – Hugh Johnson (Nelson, U.K.; Simon & Schuster, U.S.A.)

Wine regions of the world
and note pages
for what you buy and taste

WINE REGIONS OF THE WORLD

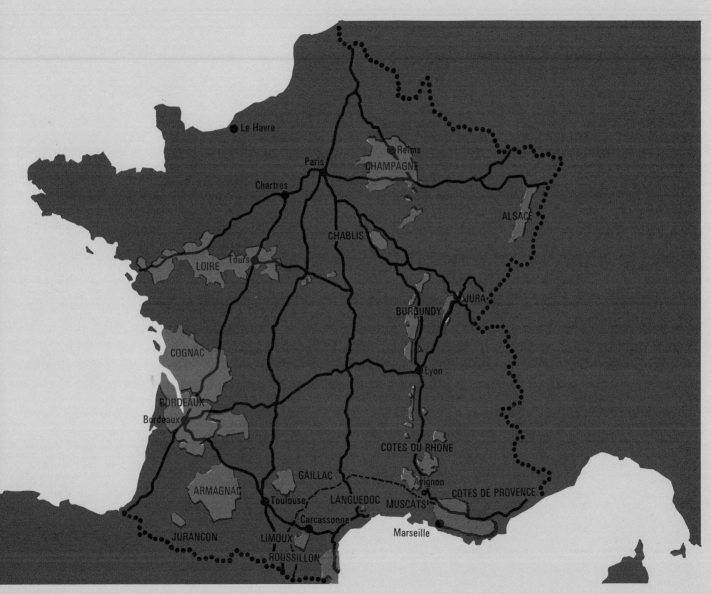

Le Havre

Reims
CHAMPAGNE

Paris

Chartres

ALSACE

CHABLIS

LOIRE
Tours

BURGUNDY

JURA

COGNAC

Lyon

BORDEAUX
Bordeaux

COTES DU RHONE

GAILLAC

Avignon

ARMAGNAC

COTES DE PROVENCE

Toulouse

LANGUEDOC

MUSCATS

Carcassonne

JURANCON

LIMOUX

Marseille

ROUSSILLON

FRANCE

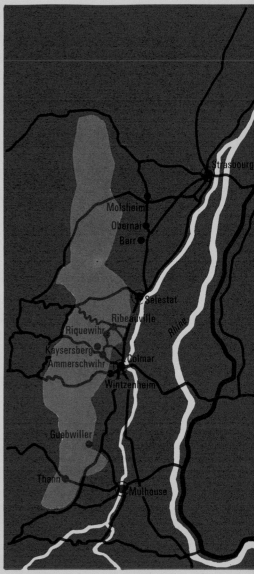

BORDEAUX

ALSACE

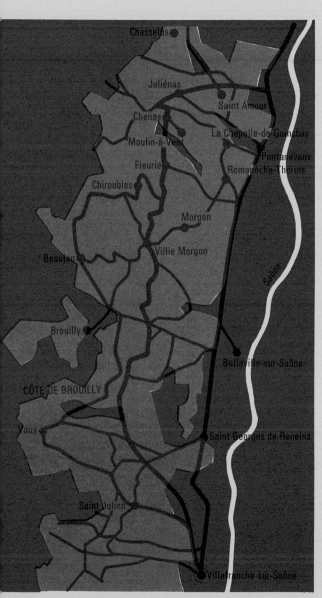

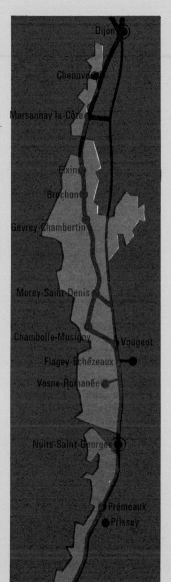

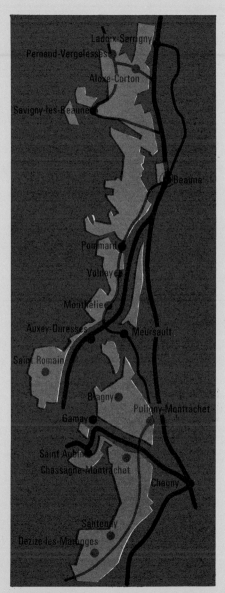

BEAUJOLAIS

BURGUNDY Côte de Nuits, Côte de Beaune

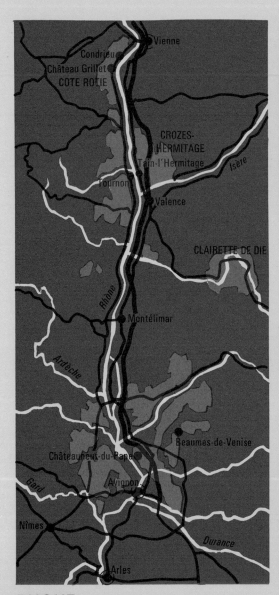

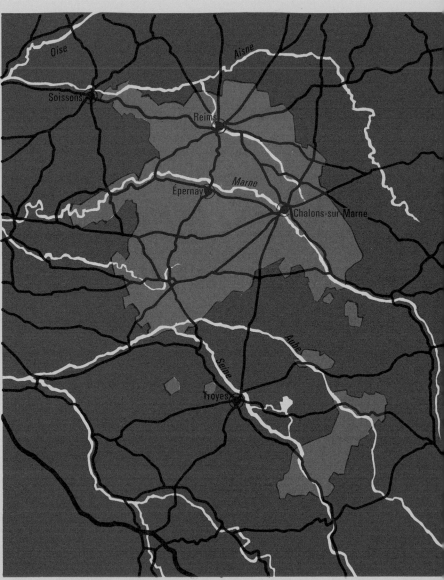

RHONE   CHAMPAGNE

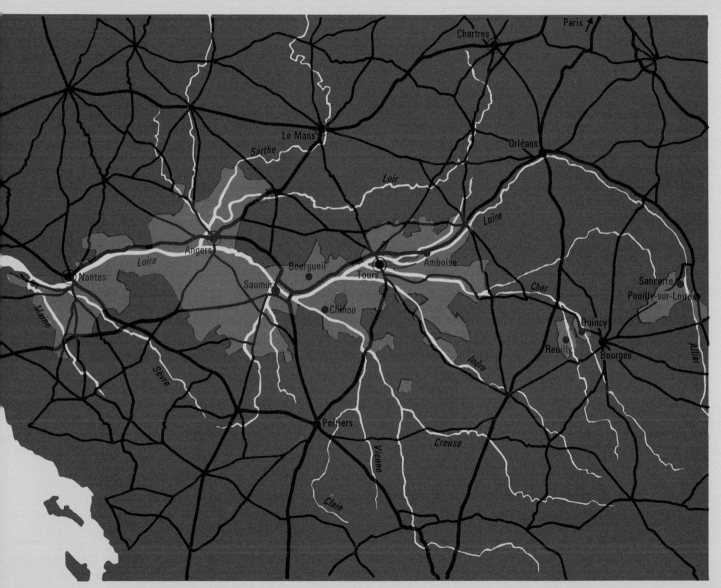

Paris →

Chartres

Le Mans

Sarthe

Loir

Orléans

Loire

Angers

Loire

Bourgueil

Amboise

Tours

Cher

Sancerre
Pouilly-sur-Loire

Nantes

Saumur

Quincy

Chinon

Reuilly

Bourges

Marne

Indre

Allier

Sèvre

Poitiers

Creuse

Vienne

Clain

LOIRE

MOSELLE AND RHINE

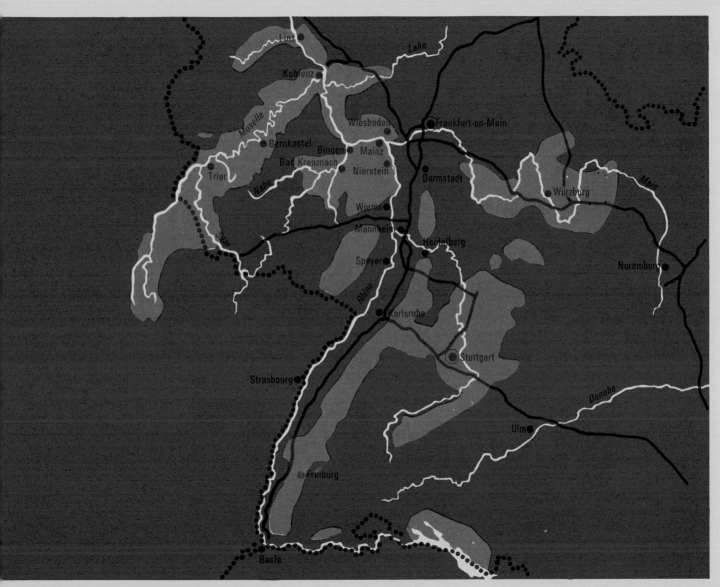

GERMAN WINE REGIONS

TRENTINO-ALTO ADIGE

● Trento

VENEZIA GIULIA

LOMBARDY

VENETO

● Trieste

Milan ●

● Venice

Turin ●

PIEDMONT

LIGURIA

Genoa

EMILIA ROMAGNA

● Bologna

Florence ●

Ancona ●

TUSCANY

THE MARCHES

Perugia ●

UMBRIA

CORSICA

LAZIO

L'Aquila ●

Rome ●

ABRUZZI MOLISE

NORTHERN ITALY

Wine is made throughout the country

Rome

ABRUZZI MOLISE

LAZIO

Naples
CAMPANIA

Bari

APULIA

Potenza

LUCANIA

CALABRIA

Reggio di Calabria

Palermo

SICILY

SOUTHERN ITALY

PORTUGAL AND SPAIN

Wine is made throughout the country

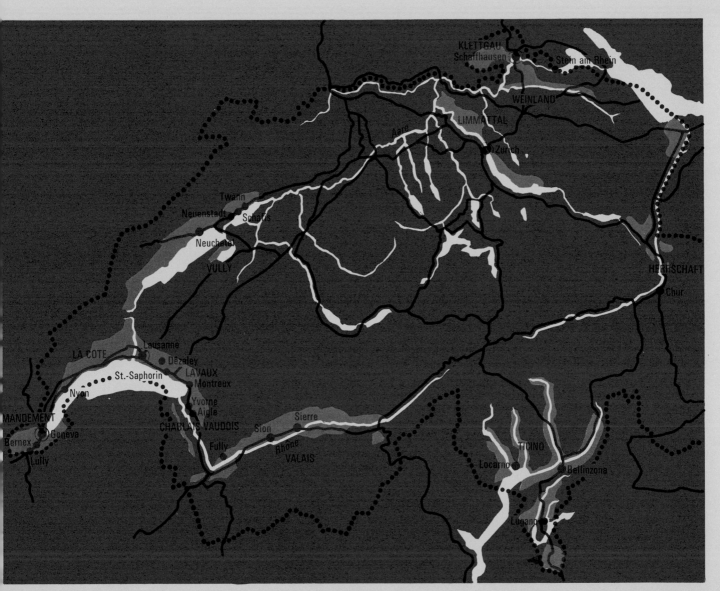

KLETTGAU
Schaffhausen
Stein am Rhein
WEINLAND
LIMMATTAL
Aare
Zürich
Twann
Neuenstadt
Schafis
HERRSCHAFT
Neuchâtel
Chur
VULLY
Lausanne
LA CÔTE
Dézaley
St.-Saphorin
LAVAUX
Nyon
Montreux
Yvorne
Aigle
Sierre
MANDEMENT
Sion
TICINO
Bernex
Geneva
Fully
Rhône
Locarno
Bellinzona
Lully
CHABLAIS VAUDOIS
VALAIS
Lugano

SWITZERLAND

AUSTRALIA

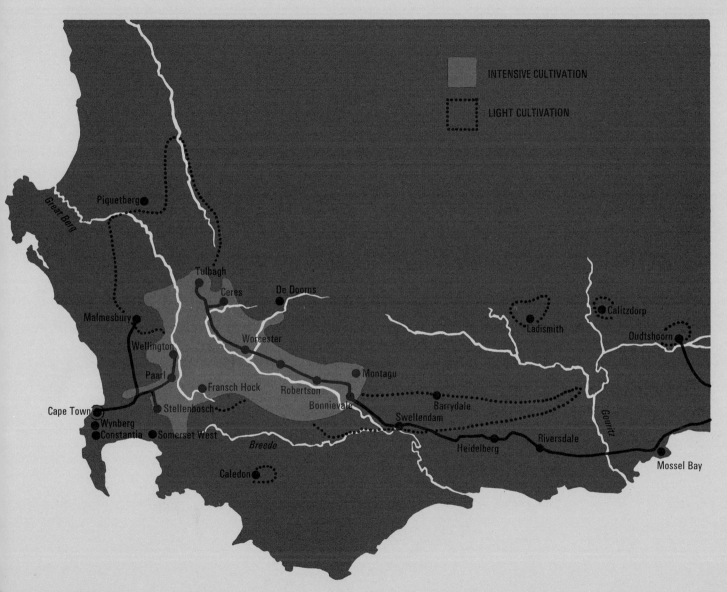

Great Berg

Piquetberg

Tulbagh

Ceres

De Doorns

Malmesbury

Wellington

Worcester

Ladismith

Calitzdorp

Oudtshoorn

Paarl

Fransch Hock

Robertson

Montagu

Cape Town

Stellenbosch

Bonnievale

Barrydale

Wynberg

Swellendam

Constantia

Somerset West

Breede

Heidelberg

Riversdale

Gouritz

Mossel Bay

Caledon

SOUTH AFRICA

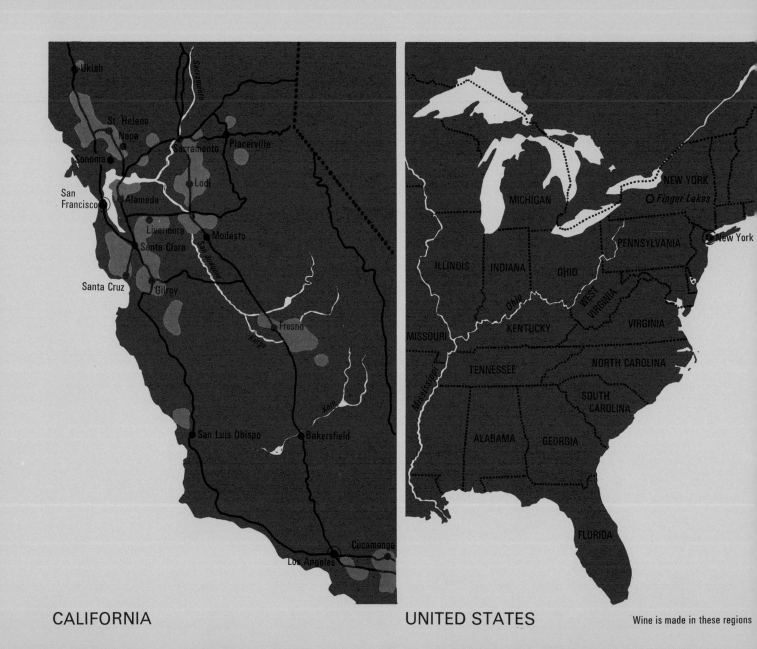

CALIFORNIA

UNITED STATES

Wine is made in these regions

NAME OF WINE	NAME OF SUPPLIER	DATE BOUGHT	PRICE	DATE OPENED	REMARKS

NAME OF WINE	NAME OF SUPPLIER	DATE BOUGHT	PRICE	DATE OPENED	REMARKS

NAME OF WINE	NAME OF SUPPLIER	DATE BOUGHT	PRICE	DATE OPENED	REMARKS

NAME OF WINE	NAME OF SUPPLIER	DATE BOUGHT	PRICE	DATE OPENED	REMARKS

NAME OF WINE	NAME OF SUPPLIER	DATE BOUGHT	PRICE	DATE OPENED	REMARKS

NAME OF WINE	NAME OF SUPPLIER	DATE BOUGHT	PRICE	DATE OPENED	REMARKS

NAME OF WINE	NAME OF SUPPLIER	DATE BOUGHT	PRICE	DATE OPENED	REMARKS

NAME OF WINE	NAME OF SUPPLIER	DATE BOUGHT	PRICE	DATE OPENED	REMARKS

NAME OF WINE	NAME OF SUPPLIER	DATE BOUGHT	PRICE	DATE OPENED	REMARKS

NAME OF WINE	NAME OF SUPPLIER	DATE BOUGHT	PRICE	DATE OPENED	REMARKS

NAME OF WINE	NAME OF SUPPLIER	DATE BOUGHT	PRICE	DATE OPENED	REMARKS

NAME OF WINE	NAME OF SUPPLIER	DATE BOUGHT	PRICE	DATE OPENED	REMARKS

NAME OF WINE	NAME OF SUPPLIER	DATE BOUGHT	PRICE	DATE OPENED	REMARKS

NAME OF WINE	NAME OF SUPPLIER	DATE BOUGHT	PRICE	DATE OPENED	REMARKS

NAME OF WINE	NAME OF SUPPLIER	DATE BOUGHT	PRICE	DATE OPENED	REMARKS

NAME OF WINE	NAME OF SUPPLIER	DATE BOUGHT	PRICE	DATE OPENED	REMARKS

NAME OF WINE	NAME OF SUPPLIER	DATE BOUGHT	PRICE	DATE OPENED	REMARKS

NAME OF WINE	NAME OF SUPPLIER	DATE BOUGHT	PRICE	DATE OPENED	REMARKS

NAME OF WINE	NAME OF SUPPLIER	DATE BOUGHT	PRICE	DATE OPENED	REMARKS

NAME OF WINE	NAME OF SUPPLIER	DATE BOUGHT	PRICE	DATE OPENED	REMARKS

NAME OF WINE	NAME OF SUPPLIER	DATE BOUGHT	PRICE	DATE OPENED	REMARKS

NAME OF WINE	NAME OF SUPPLIER	DATE BOUGHT	PRICE	DATE OPENED	REMARKS

NAME OF WINE	NAME OF SUPPLIER	DATE BOUGHT	PRICE	DATE OPENED	REMARKS

NAME OF WINE	NAME OF SUPPLIER	DATE BOUGHT	PRICE	DATE OPENED	REMARKS

NAME OF WINE	NAME OF SUPPLIER	DATE BOUGHT	PRICE	DATE OPENED	REMARKS

NAME OF WINE	NAME OF SUPPLIER	DATE BOUGHT	PRICE	DATE OPENED	REMARKS

NAME OF WINE	NAME OF SUPPLIER	DATE BOUGHT	PRICE	DATE OPENED	REMARKS

NAME OF WINE	NAME OF SUPPLIER	DATE BOUGHT	PRICE	DATE OPENED	REMARKS

NAME OF WINE	NAME OF SUPPLIER	DATE BOUGHT	PRICE	DATE OPENED	REMARKS

NAME OF WINE	NAME OF SUPPLIER	DATE BOUGHT	PRICE	DATE OPENED	REMARKS

NAME OF WINE	NAME OF SUPPLIER	DATE BOUGHT	PRICE	DATE OPENED	REMARKS

NAME OF WINE	NAME OF SUPPLIER	DATE BOUGHT	PRICE	DATE OPENED	REMARKS